PROTECTION
from
DECEPTION

DEREK PRINCE

WHITAKER
HOUSE

Publisher's Note:
This book was compiled from the extensive archive of Derek Prince's unpublished materials and approved by the Derek Prince Ministries editorial team.

PROTECTION FROM DECEPTION

Derek Prince Ministries
P.O. Box 19501
Charlotte, North Carolina 28219
www.derekprince.org

ISBN: 978-0-88368-230-2
ISBN: 0-88368-230-3
Printed in the United States of America
© 2008 by Derek Prince Ministries, International

Whitaker House
1030 Hunt Valley Circle
New Kensington, PA 15068
www.whitakerhouse.com

Library of Congress Cataloging-in Publication Data
Prince, Derek.
Protection from deception / by Derek Prince.
p.   cm.
Summary: "Prepares Christians to be on their guard against deception by satanic forces and to remain members of the true church, the bride of Christ, at the end of the age"—Provided by publisher.
ISBN 978-0-88368-230-2 (trade pbk. : alk. paper) 1. Discernment (Christian theology) 2. Spiritual warfare. I. Title.
BV4509.5.P75 2008
234'.13—dc22   2007048482

1 2 3 4 5 6 7 8 9 10 11 12 **WH** 16 15 14 13 12 11 10 09 08

CONTENTS

INTRODUCTION

In recent years, the church has witnessed a worldwide surge in signs and wonders—some biblical and helpful, others unbiblical and bizarre. Signs and wonders are not new phenomena; they are recorded in various Scripture passages and have been reported in different periods of church history. They extend beyond a specific church or denomination and have received attention from the religious and secular media alike.

I harbor no personal prejudice or skepticism about unusual manifestations, primarily because I have experienced a number of such phenomena in my life, starting with my own conversion experience while I was serving with the British army in World War II. I will expound upon this in the first chapter.

One should not accept every unusual manifestation indiscriminately, however. Two questions should always qualify every such manifestation. First, is it a manifestation of the Holy Spirit of God or of some other source? Second, is the manifestation in harmony with Scripture, or does it contradict the Word of God? As Paul attested in 2 Timothy 3:16,

"All Scripture is given by inspiration of God." The Holy Spirit authored all of Scripture, and He never contradicts Himself. Therefore, every genuine manifestation of the Holy Spirit must concur with Scripture.

I once had close contact with a group claiming to experience supernatural manifestations. The group leaders were enthusiastic about the wonderful things they experienced at their meetings, but when they invited us to join them, they instructed us not to test or examine them, but to simply open up to receive them. This uncritical stance made me wary of this group's experience, because their method of acceptance without evaluation directly contradicts scriptural instruction. In 1 Thessalonians 5:21, Paul told believers to *"test all things; hold fast what is good."* Failure to test supernatural experiences is a failure to follow the mandates of Scripture.

Jesus provided distinct warnings against deception by false manifestations that will be ushered in at the end of the age. Four of these warnings are recorded within twenty-one verses in the book of Matthew. First, in Matthew 24:4, Jesus warned, *"Take heed that no one deceives you."* In verse 5, He foretold, *"For many will come in My name, saying, 'I am the Christ [Messiah],' and will deceive many."* In verse 11, He warned, *"Then many false prophets will rise up and deceive many."* Finally, in verse 24, He concluded, *"For false christs [messiahs] and false prophets will rise and show great signs and wonders to deceive, if possible, even the elect."* These warnings are not to be taken lightly. Anyone who disregards them does so at the peril of his own soul.

Deception—not sickness, poverty, or persecution—is the greatest single danger in the end of the age. Anyone who denies his vulnerability to deception is already deceived, for Jesus has foretold it and He does not err. Our hearts are incapable of discerning truth on their own. Proverbs 28:26 teaches, *"He who trusts in his own heart is a fool."* We must not be fools by trusting our hearts. Whatever our hearts tell us is unreliable, as Jeremiah 17:9 attests: *"The heart is deceitful above all things, and desperately wicked; who can know it?"* In Hebrew, the word deceitful is active rather than passive. The heart is not deceived; rather, the heart is a deceiver, leading you astray.

It is also important to realize that signs and wonders neither guarantee nor determine truth. Truth is established and unchanging; it is the Word of God. In John 17:17, Jesus prayed to the Father, *"Your word is truth."* The psalmist declared, *"Forever, O LORD, Your word is settled in heaven"* (Psalm 119:89). No event on earth, whether natural or supernatural, can change the slightest sign or letter in the Word of God.

True signs attest the truth; lying signs attest lies. Many Christians assume that every supernatural sign must be from God, forgetting that Satan, or the devil, is completely capable of performing supernatural signs and wonders. As Paul wrote in his second epistle to the Thessalonians,

> *The coming of the lawless one* [the Antichrist] *is according to the working of Satan, with all power, signs, and lying wonders, and with all unrighteous deception among those who perish, because they did not receive the love of the truth, that they might be saved. And for this reason God will send them strong delusion, that they should believe the lie, that they all may be condemned who did not believe the truth but had pleasure in unrighteousness.* (2 Thessalonians 2:9–12)

This passage proves that lying signs and wonders exist; a phenomenon is not true based solely on its classification as a supernatural manifestation. Recall that in Exodus, many of Moses' miracles before Pharaoh were matched by Pharaoh's magicians and sorcerers. (See Exodus 7:11–23.) Moses' staff-turned-serpent ultimately ate the serpents formed from the sorcerers' rods, but the fact remains that Satan can give people the power to perform certain miracles.

Those who accept Satan's lies do so *"because they did not receive the love of the truth....God will send them strong delusion"* (2 Thessalonians 2:10–11). This is among the Bible's most frightening statements. If God sends strong delusion, we are sure to be deceived. Condemnation comes to those who *"did not believe the truth but had pleasure in unrighteousness"* (verse 12).

The only way to know whether a sign or wonder is true is to measure it with truth—with the Word of God. In John 8:32, Jesus said, *"You shall know the truth, and the truth shall make you free."* Scripture is the sole determinant of truth or falsehood. We are instructed to *"test all things; hold fast what is good"* (1 Thessalonians 5:21).

The book of Revelation promises a specific series of supernatural signs and wonders that will signify the end of the age, but we must practice discernment as we anticipate judgment day, guarding ourselves against the devil's tactics and holding fast to the true church, the bride of Christ.

As we await the day when our heavenly Bridegroom, Jesus Christ, will return to deliver us fully from this present evil age, we must be set apart from the world. When the Scriptures say world, they generally refer to the world system—the political and social order that rejects God, is ruled by Satan, and governs the minds and manners of people who have not been saved. Through Jesus' death and resurrection, God secured ultimate victory over the devil. Satan may rule this world, but his reign is fast approaching its end. Our deliverance—and God's glory—shall endure for all ages. With this in mind, we are to share God's light and love with the world—not to be confused with falling in love with the world or seeking to receive its love. Focusing on our heavenly home, we must clothe ourselves with humility. We must put off all self-seeking efforts and motives. These only fuel our pride, a dangerous attitude that blinds us to Satan's deception and makes us vulnerable. And we must cling to the cross, the same instrument that deals Satan's death sentence and secures our salvation through Christ's victory.

Hallelujah Jesus

Signs, Wonders, and Unusual Manifestations

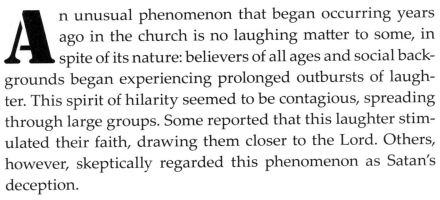

An unusual phenomenon that began occurring years ago in the church is no laughing matter to some, in spite of its nature: believers of all ages and social backgrounds began experiencing prolonged outbursts of laughter. This spirit of hilarity seemed to be contagious, spreading through large groups. Some reported that this laughter stimulated their faith, drawing them closer to the Lord. Others, however, skeptically regarded this phenomenon as Satan's deception.

People would often ask me about the source of this laughter—could it possibly come from the Holy Spirit? I would tell them this was indeed possible. (I had to believe that, because laughter is how I came to Christ. Or should I say, laughter is how Christ came to me.)

A Joyful Supernatural Conversion

In the summer of 1941, I was stationed with a medical unit of the British army in a hotel on the North Bay of Scarborough in Yorkshire, England. The hotel had been gutted of its furniture, so we slept on straw mattresses on the floor. A nominal Anglican at the time, I was reading my Bible through from beginning to end, but not for devotional purposes. Rather, I regarded the Bible as a work of philosophy. As a professional philosopher, I deemed the work important to read as my academic duty. By this point, I had reached the book of Job.

In Scarborough, I interacted on several occasions with Pentecostal Christians, who were the first people to confront me with the necessity of receiving Christ as my personal Lord and Savior. Presented by the Pentecostals with the claims of Christ, I decided one night to pray until something happened. I did not know what to expect, but starting at eleven o'clock, I struggled for one hour to form a coherent prayer. Around midnight, I was distinctly aware of a divine presence with me and found myself repeating the words Jacob articulated to the Man with whom he wrestled at Peniel: *"I will not let You go unless You bless me!"* (Genesis 32:26).

With increasing emphasis, I repeated, "I will not let You go, I will not let You go," until I added, "Make me love You more and more…more and more and more…."

An invisible power came over me, and I found myself lying face-up on the floor with my arms in the air, repeating, "More and more and more…." Moments later, my words turned to deep sobs that rose up in my stomach and then shook my body before escaping through my lips. Half an hour later, an indescribable and involuntary change occurred: my sobbing turned to laughter. Like the sobs, the laughter proceeded from my stomach. Gentle at first, it gradually grew louder, reverberating off the walls of the room.

The soldier who shared my room woke up to find me on my back, laughing uproariously with my arms in the air. He cast me several helpless glances and said, "I don't know what to do with you. I suppose it's no good pouring water over you." Within me, an inaudible response arose: "Even water would not put this out!" Not wanting to disturb my fellow soldier, I crawled to my mattress, pulled a blanket over my head, and laughed myself to sleep. I knew that the Holy Spirit was within me.

When I awoke the next morning, I was a totally different person. No longer did vile language flow from my mouth. Prayer was effortless; it came as naturally to me as breathing. I could do nothing—not even drink a glass of water—without thanking God. At six o'clock that evening, I headed to the pub for my customary drink; however, it seemed as if my legs locked at the door, and I could not enter. I stopped trying to move my legs when I realized the pub's fare no longer tempted me.

I returned to my billet and opened my Bible, which had become a new book overnight. It seemed as if God and I were the only two people in the universe. God spoke directly to me through the Bible text. I opened to Psalm 126:1–2, which reads, *"When the LORD brought back the captivity of Zion, we were like those who dream. Then our mouth was filled with laughter."* That's exactly what happened to me, I thought. *It wasn't I who was laughing. My mouth was being filled with laughter from some other source!*

Supernatural laughter expressed the joy of God's people when He delivered them from captivity.

Upon further reflection, I realized that this strange, supernatural laughter expressed the same joy and excitement of God's people when He delivered them from captivity.

In Job, I came across another relevant passage: *"Behold, God will not cast away the blameless....He will yet fill your mouth with laughing, and your lips with rejoicing"* (Job 8:20–21). This laughter does not result from a person's own will; it comes from God Himself as a response to the assurance of His acceptance.

God's Laughter

In the book of Psalms, I made another discovery: God Himself laughs. His laughter is not, however, a reaction to something comical, but rather an expression of triumph over His enemies. When a wicked man plots against a righteous man, *"The*

God laughs as an expression of triumph over His enemies.

Lord laughs at him, for He sees that his day is coming" (Psalm 37:13).

When earthly rulers scorn God's government, *"He who sits in the heavens shall laugh; the Lord shall hold them in derision"* (Psalm 2:4). Regarding the evils of unregenerate men, the psalmist writes, *"But You, O Lord, shall laugh at them; You shall have all the nations in derision"* (Psalm 59:8). The righteous can join in God's jubilation: *"The righteous also shall see and fear, and shall laugh at him* [the wicked, evil man]*"* (Psalm 52:6).

In addition to explaining the source of my laughter, the Bible shed light on the identity of the Person from whom I was requesting blessing: Jesus of Nazareth, the same Man

Jacob encountered at Peniel. Jacob met Him before His incarnation; I met Him after His resurrection. Both man and God, this Person could have been none other than Jesus of Nazareth.

About ten days after my first encounter with the Lord, I was lying on my mattress in the barrack when I started speaking an unfamiliar language that sounded like Chinese. I recalled what I had heard in church about speaking with other tongues. At first, I spoke with timidity. As I relaxed, the words came freely, with forcefulness. They did not originate in my mind or mouth, but in my stomach, like the sobs and laughter.

The next evening, I spoke again in an unknown language—this time, it was different from the previous instance. The words possessed a marked, poetic rhythm. After a brief silence, I spoke again—in English. The words did not originate in my mind, however, and their rhythm seemed to mirror that of the previously uttered speech. I concluded that what I was speaking in English was an interpretive rendering of what I had spoken in an unknown tongue.

Unconventional, but Not Unbiblical

While my laughter was an unconventional spiritual experience, it was no less authentic. In Matthew 12:33, Jesus explained the test for spiritual experience: *"A tree is known by its fruit."* What was the fruit of my strange experience? A life converted from sin to righteousness, from agnostic dabbling in the occult to an unshakable faith in Jesus Christ as revealed in Scripture; a life that has brought forth fruit in God's kingdom. Since this experience, I have had several additional instances of supernatural laughter. I have even seen God

15

touch other believers in a similar way. Supernatural laughter cleanses and exhilarates, and it has even prompted miracles of physical healing and deliverance from emotional burdens such as depression.

A second example from my experiences with unusual manifestations occurred while I was a pastor in London. One evening, I was praying with some people from our fellowship on the top floor of a four-story building when the building suddenly shuddered and shook for thirty minutes—it shook with the power of God. At this time, a lame man was miraculously healed and threw away his crutches. It was at this very time that they began to praise God and the building started to shake.

A similar sign in the early church was recorded by Luke in Acts 4:31:

When they had prayed, the place where they were assembled together was shaken; and they were all filled with the Holy Spirit, and they spoke the word of God with boldness.

The Biblical Record

The simple fact that something is unconventional or unusual should not provoke automatic wariness, for it may indeed be from God. In the Old Testament, God's prophets did some unusual things. Isaiah had to walk barefoot and naked for three years. (See Isaiah 20:1–4.) Ezekiel was required to lie on his left side for three hundred and ninety days and on his right side for forty days; he had to prepare his food on a fire of cow dung. (See Ezekiel 4:4–15.)

In the gospels, Jesus Himself healed people in unconventional ways. He healed a deaf mute by spitting and touching the man's tongue. (See Mark 7:32–35.) He healed a blind man by making clay from His own spittle and smearing it on his eyes. (See John 9:6–7.) In the book of Acts, many features and events of the early church are unconventional compared to the church today.

Events from History

Unusual manifestations have long characterized the ministries of well-known spiritual leaders, including John Wesley, George Whitefield, Jonathan Edwards, and Charles Finney. Their ministries differed from the current trend in unusual manifestations, however.

First, the principal activity of these men was preaching God's Word. It was not unusual for Finney to preach a two-hour message; today, most sermons are significantly abridged to suit the short attention span of listeners.

Second, these men made a fervent call to repentance. A penitent spirit preceded the change; the same should occur today, but people clamor for "a refreshing" without realizing the prerequisite of repentance, which Peter articulated in Acts 3:19: *"Repent therefore and be converted, that your sins may be blotted out, so that times of refreshing may come from the presence of the Lord."*

In the Christian church, supernatural activity should be regarded with neither blind faith nor cynical skepticism. We are instructed to *"test all things; hold fast what is good"* (1 Thessalonians 5:21). We must apply Scripture to test any sign, as Hebrews 5:14 indicates: *"But solid food is for the mature, who by constant use have trained themselves to distinguish good from evil"* (NIV). Discernment and a diet of solid spiritual food will enable us to assess the authenticity of signs we encounter.

17

Five Movements That Went Astray

Some movements start with a genuine prompting of the Holy Spirit, but they veer off track, straying from the truths of Scripture and ignoring God's guidance. I would like to review five examples. Within the overarching charismatic movement are five specific movements with which I have had a personal association that raise questions about their legitimacy and authenticity.

The Latter Rain

In the Canadian province of Saskatchewan shortly after World War II, an outpouring of the Holy Spirit came to be called the "Latter Rain." Many people emigrated from the United States to Saskatchewan, and the lasting effect of this movement was a restoration of the gifts of the Holy Spirit. About one decade later, from 1957 to 1962, I was a missionary with the Pentecostal Assemblies of Canada, and I inquired why the members of the Pentecostal Assemblies seldom—if ever—exercised spiritual gifts. They told me that "Latter Rain" had the spiritual gifts; in other words, because Latter Rain possessed the gifts and went astray, they did not want the gifts because they feared they might do the same. This notion is unfounded and the people showed signs of being deceived. In addition, the leaders became proud and self-assertive, falling into immorality.

The Manifest Sons of God

Another example is the Manifest Sons of God, a persuasive group of men who strongly believed the Scripture that all creation is waiting for the manifestation of the sons of

18

God. (See Romans 8:19 KJV.) Their ministry was powerful, particularly in casting out demons. But they would engage in prolonged conversations with these demons, seeking revelation from them. Seeking revelation from demons is unscriptural, as was their theological conviction that some members of their group had already received their resurrection bodies. (See 2 Timothy 2:18.)

The Children of God

Next were the "Children of God," who changed their name to "The Family." Their female leader was powerful and captivating, but she manipulated the minds of young people, undermining relationships with their parents and families.

William Branham

William Branham had a remarkable ministry with incredible scope. He was a gentle, humble man with a legendary ministry of the word of knowledge. Once, at a meeting in Phoenix, Arizona, he chose a woman in the audience from his position on the platform and told her, "Now, you're not here for yourself. You're here for your grandson." Next, he said her name and street address in New York City—it was all accurate.

On several occasions, after exercising his gift, Branham collapsed and was carried offstage. Ern Baxter, the Bible teacher at Branham's evangelistic meetings and a colleague of mine, once told me in private that "Branham had two spirits; one was the Spirit of God, one was not." After Branham died in an automobile accident, his followers embalmed his body and kept it unburied until Easter Sunday, many months later, when they thought he would be resurrected. He was not.

Discipleship, or the Shepherding Movement

Lastly, "Discipleship" or the "Shepherding Movement" began with the genuine, supernatural intervention of God. During a convention, three fellow preachers—Bob Mumford, Charles Simpson, and Don Basham—and I discovered that the man who was leading the convention was a practicing homosexual. We met to pray about how to address the situation, and by the time our prayer was finished, we knew that God had joined the four of us together. Subsequently, we made a commitment to cover one another in prayer, to submit our personal lives to one another's scrutiny, and to confer together before making any major personal decisions.

Later, however, selfish ambition took control and inexperienced men were being put in positions of authority. In addition, our minds were not renewed, nor were we unified in purpose or aligned with God's purpose.

There are some common threads running through all five of these movements. One is pride, which I consider the most dangerous sin. Proverbs 16:18 wisely warns, *"Pride goes before destruction, and a haughty spirit before a fall."* The second common thread is a mixture of spirits—truth and error, the Holy Spirit and other spirits. These other spirits enter during a person's decline from earthly to soulish to demonic (see James 3:15), concepts we will discuss at length in later chapters.

TESTING

MOVEMENTS

WITHIN THE CHURCH

Every trend or movement in the church must be tested to determine whether it is from God. I have emphasized the biblical principle that *"a tree is known by its fruit"* (Matthew 12:33). I have witnessed people who were "drunk" or "intoxicated" in the Spirit, but I always look for the fruit. What comes from these experiences of intoxication and other unusual states?

In the New Testament church, supernatural signs were always designed to follow and affirm the preaching of God's Word. In Mark 16:17–18, Jesus told the disciples, Follow

These signs will follow those who believe: in My name they will cast out demons; they will speak with new tongues; they will take up serpents; and if they drink anything deadly, it will by no means hurt them; they will lay hands on the sick, and they will recover.

Movements from God bear fruit that identifies them as such. The following are five primary fruits by which we can authenticate present moves in the church.

21

The Fruit of Repentance

In the New Testament, God demands repentance more than He demands faith. John the Baptist prepared the way for Jesus by calling people to repent. (See Matthew 3:2.) Anyone he baptized was required to first bear the fruit of repentance (see verses 7–8). When Jesus came, the first recorded word He preached was *"Repent."* (See, for example, Mark 1:15.) He instructed the multitudes, *"Unless you repent you will all likewise perish"* (Luke 13:3).

True repentance is a decision of the will.

After His resurrection, Jesus told the disciples that when they preached to the nations, they should teach that repentance precedes forgiveness of sins. (See Luke 24:47.) Paul's ministry reflected the same priority: speaking in Athens, he said, *"God...now commands all men everywhere to repent"* (Acts 17:30).

What constitutes true repentance? It is not an emotion but a decision of the will—a decision to turn away from sin and unrighteousness and to submit unreservedly to the lordship of Jesus Christ. Repentance is first among the six foundational doctrines listed in Hebrews 6:1–2.

Without true repentance, no one can build his life as a Christian on a solid foundation. I have counseled hundreds of Christians through various problems, and I have reached the conclusion that at least half of the problems come from the failure to truly repent.

The church has an urgent need to place renewed emphasis on repentance and on the confession of sins. Years ago, I was invited to speak in Hull, a small city in England. A

22

group of leaders representing about fifteen churches had been meeting together for years to wait on God. They invited me to speak to them. These meetings differed from most others I attended because of their unique atmosphere. I preached a straight message, the gist of which was, *"If you need to confess sins, you can confess them to God, but the Bible also says to confess your sins to one another, that you may be healed."* (See James 5:16.) Once I invited those present to come to the platform to confess their sins, they came streaming down one by one for about two hours. To me, this was significant. I saw it as the fruit that comes when we are waiting on God.

Sin that we do not confess becomes a formidable barrier to revival. Until we confess our sins, all the preaching and praise songs in the world will produce no effect. We often think, "I do not have any sins that I know of." But if we wait a little on the Lord, He will often reveal them to us.

I once read in the journals of John Wesley about a strong Methodist Society in Yorkshire made up of people who would meet weekly to confess their sins to one another. This is hardly the modern plan for starting a church. But James 5:16 instructs us, *"Confess your trespasses to one another, and pray for one another, that you may be healed."*

We must walk with one another in fellowship, confessing our sins.

We have access to God through the cleansing blood of Jesus, but first we have to walk in the light—we must walk with one another in fellowship, confessing our sins. If we are out of fellowship, we are out of the light, because walking in the light entails fellowship. Jesus' blood cleanses not in the dark, but in the light; thus, fellowship and confession of sins are crucial to being cleansed by Christ's blood. (See 1 John 1:9.)

The Fruit of Respect for Scripture

Jesus called Scripture *"the word of God"* (see, for example, Mark 7:13; Luke 8:11), and He set His seal upon it with five simple words: *"the Scripture cannot be broken"* (John 10:35). If we believe in Jesus, we believe in the Bible. By the same token, if we do not believe the Bible, we do not believe Jesus, either. In Isaiah 66:2, the Lord says, *"This is the one I esteem: he who is humble and contrite in spirit, and trembles at my word"* (NIV). Here God combines repentance—a humble and contrite spirit—with a fearful respect for His Word.

> *The Holy Spirit draws believers around the person of Jesus.*

Why should we tremble at God's Word? There are many reasons, but here—briefly—are two important ones. First, God's Word is the way through which God the Father and God the Son come and make their home with us. (See John 14:23.) Second, we will ultimately be judged by God's Word. (See John 12:48.)

From the beginning of creation, God has worked through two agents: His Word and His Spirit. The Spirit of God moved first; then, God's Word went forth (see Genesis 1:2–3). Creation was the result. God's Spirit and God's Word work together in harmony. God's Spirit acts according to God's Word, and Scripture—God's Word—is inspired by the Holy Spirit.

God never contradicts Himself. Thus, every spiritual manifestation must be tested according to Scripture. (See 2 Timothy 3:16.) Anything that does not correspond to Scripture must be rejected.

The Fruit of Exalting Jesus

In John 16:13–14, Jesus promised His disciples, *"When He, the Spirit of truth, has come, He will guide you into all truth.... He will glorify Me."* This passage reveals two important facts about the ministry of the Holy Spirit. First, His supreme function is to glorify Jesus. Any authentic spiritual manifestation also glorifies Jesus, focusing our attention on Him alone.

When human personality takes the stage and assumes supremacy, the Holy Spirit starts to withdraw. Exalting human personalities instead of the Holy Spirit has often inhibited genuine moves of the Holy Spirit. Churches sometimes err when they replace Christ, the church's true Head, with a pastor or parish leader.

Pastors are wonderful people, but they cannot take the place of Jesus. The chief function of pastors is not to solve your problems but to help you cultivate your relationship with Jesus, the Head. Some people mistakenly make pastors their go-to people, assuming they have all the right answers. Some pastors overstep their place and wrongly control their congregations. They may even claim to be necessary channels of communication with Christ.

Years ago, I knew a successful, godly pastor in Sweden who had built the largest Pentecostal church in Europe. From time to time, he would say to his congregation, "Please do not put me on a pedestal. For if you do, God will have to let

25

me fall." Charismatic personalities who occupy a pedestal incur the jealousy of God, who says in Isaiah 48:11, *"I will not give My glory to another."*

It is true that we must have spiritual mentors. But more importantly, we must also have a personal relationship with Christ—one that enables us to hear His voice, discern His guidance, and know what pleases and angers Him. We must be sensitive to our Head.

Second, John 16:13–14 highlights the Holy Spirit's identity by using the pronoun "He" rather than "it." Just as Jesus is a person, so too the Holy Spirit is a person who draws believers together around the person of Jesus. When people describe their spiritual life as experiencing "it," rather than using a personal pronoun for Jesus or the Holy Spirit, they refer to the wrong thing.

The Fruit of Love for Fellow Christians

In John 13:35, Jesus told His followers, *"By this all will know that you are My disciples, if you have love for one another."* The apostle Paul echoed this truth in 1 Timothy 1:5: *"The goal of our instruction is love from a pure heart and a good conscience and a sincere faith"* (NASB).

Any "religious" activity not characterized by love and community Paul dismissed as *"fruitless discussion"* (verse 6 NASB). In 1 Corinthians 13:2, Paul also pointed to the importance of love: *"If I have the gift of prophecy and can fathom all mysteries and all knowledge, and if I have a faith that can move mountains, but have not love, I am nothing"* (NIV). Each of us must ask: Has my faith made me a loving person?

The church must undergo a similar interrogation. When a move of the Holy Spirit occurs, we must ask: Does it produce Christians who sincerely love one another, regardless of denominational labels? Does the movement cause such love that unbelievers wonder in amazement at the community and compassion of Christians?

The Fruit of Loving Concern for the Unreached

Jesus told His disciples in John 4:35, *"Lift up your eyes and look at the fields, for they are already white for harvest!"* If these words were true in Jesus' day, their truth is even more urgent today. Based on extensive travel and worldwide ministry, I have come to the conclusion that we are living in the harvest hour. Many Christians who could be working in the harvest fields of the world are instead entangled in the snare of materialistic self-centeredness. A genuine move of the Holy Spirit must release a multitude of new laborers into the harvest fields.

Does the Church Pass the Test?

If a significant number of Christians in a given movement pass most or all of the five tests I just described, we can safely conclude that it is indeed a genuine move of God. This does not mean, however, that everyone or everything in the move is without blemish or flaw. None of God's people is faultless, but God is amazing in what He accomplishes with weak and fallible people when they surrender to Him.

THE IDENTITY
OF THE HOLY SPIRIT

We need to be able to recognize the Holy Spirit. Then we will know when He is moving in the church—and when He is absent. The Bible introduces the triune Godhead in Genesis 1:1–2: *"In the beginning God created the heavens and the earth. The earth was without form, and void; and darkness was on the face of the deep. And the Spirit of God was hovering over the face of the waters."* We are first introduced not to the Father or to the Son, but to the Holy Spirit, who was *"hovering over the face of the waters."* The Holy Spirit moved with creative power on behalf of the Godhead, and this creative role carried through the formation of the earth and everything in it.

Genesis 1:3 says, *"God said, 'Let there be light'; and there was light."* Psalm 33:6 tells us, *"By the word of the Lord the heavens were made, and all the host of them by the breath* [Spirit] *of His mouth."* God's creative power was channeled through His word and His Spirit, which executed His pronouncement.

God's Unique Motive

The Hebrew name for God in Genesis 1, *Elohim*, is plural. *Im* in Hebrew serves the same function as adding *s, es,* or *i* to

29

the ends of words in English to make them plural. The verb for *"created,"* *bara*, is singular, presenting a significant paradox between a plural subject and singular verb.

God is one, and yet He is more than one; He is simultaneously plural and singular. This truth is immediately introduced to us by the first three words of the Bible (in the Hebrew text) and runs throughout the Scriptures, shedding light on God's triune identity.

It is significant that God's Holy Spirit is the first person of the Godhead we encounter in the Bible. I believe that when we develop a personal relationship with God, initial contact is made not by the Father or the Son, but by the Holy Spirit, who introduces us to the Son.

Reflecting on our experiences as Christians, many of us will recognize that before we came to know Jesus, another influence was at work in our lives. Our way of thinking and our desires started to shift. We may have grown disenchanted with the way things were. This was no one but the Spirit of God stirring our hearts and preparing us for God's Word, which brings light.

Cooperation with the Father and the Son

God's Holy Spirit has a special role in the process of redemption. In every stage, Father, Son, and Holy Spirit cooperate to perform crucial acts.

The process of redemption began with Jesus' incarnation, explained in Matthew 1:18: *"The birth of Jesus Christ was as follows: After His mother Mary was betrothed to Joseph, before they came together, she was found with child of the Holy Spirit."* Luke 1:34–35 describes Mary's incredulity and the angel Gabriel's response:

30

Then Mary said to the angel, "How can this be, since I do not know a man?" And the angel answered and said to her, "The Holy Spirit will come upon you, and the power of the Highest will overshadow you; therefore, also, that Holy One who is to be born will be called the Son of God."

The Holy Spirit actually formed the infant Jesus within Mary's womb.

The Holy Spirit also played a key role in Jesus' miracles and ministry on earth. At the house of Cornelius after Jesus' death and resurrection, Peter summarized His ministry in one verse: *"God anointed Jesus of Nazareth with the Holy Spirit and with power, who went about doing good and healing all who were oppressed by the devil, for God was with Him"* (Acts 10:38). The Father, Son, and Spirit work together to help humanity, to heal the sick, and to defeat the devil.

Father, Son, and Holy Spirit work together to defeat the devil.

Regarding Jesus' death on the cross, Hebrews 9:14 says, *"Christ…through the eternal Spirit* [the Holy Spirit] *offered Himself without spot to God."* Again, we see three persons working together: Christ the Son offered Himself through the Holy Spirit to the Father.

The same is true of the resurrection: Paul recorded in Romans 1:3–4 that Jesus *"was born of the seed of David according to the flesh, and declared to be the Son of God with power according to the Spirit of holiness, by the resurrection from the dead."* Thus, the power that raised Jesus from the dead was the Holy Spirit.

Acts 2 describes Pentecost, when the Holy Spirit descended upon the disciples and caused them to speak in tongues. Peter, addressing the crowd, preached a sermon centered on the life, ministry, death, and resurrection of Jesus. Acts 2:32–33 says,

This Jesus God has raised up, of which we are all witnesses. Therefore being exalted to the right hand of God, and having received from the Father the promise of the Holy Spirit, He poured out this which you now see and hear.

At Pentecost, the Son received the Spirit from the Father and poured out the Spirit on the waiting disciples. Thus, Father, Son, and Holy Spirit work together for the good of humanity, effecting our redemption and salvation.

The Impact of the Spirit

Psalm 14:1–3 depicts a man whose heart is devoid of the Holy Spirit:

The fool has said in his heart, "There is no God." They are corrupt, they have done abominable works, there is none who does good. The LORD looks down from heaven upon the children of men, to see if there are any who understand, who seek God. They have all turned aside, they have together become corrupt; there is none who does good, no, not one.

When the Spirit of God is absent, man's heart neither seeks God nor knows it should. The Holy Spirit alone fills people with a longing for the truth. It is only by His grace that people turn from sin, humble themselves, seek God, and place their faith in Him.

The Holy Spirit alone can impart holiness, which is necessary in salvation. The work of the Holy Spirit does not stop there, though. In Ephesians 2:18, Paul explained that God indwells the church of Jesus Christ, His people who have been redeemed: *"Through Him* [Jesus] *we…have access by one Spirit to the Father."*

We have access to the Father through Jesus the Son by the Spirit—neither by doctrine nor by eloquent words. These will ascend no higher than the church roof without help from the Holy Spirit. No one approaches God except through the Holy Spirit. All Christians need a relationship with Him, something many of them lamentably seem to lack.

The Holy Spirit Is a Person

We must understand that the Holy Spirit is as much a person as God the Father and God the Son. He is not a theological abstraction or a phrase to conclude the Apostles' Creed. He is a real person, and the course of our Christian walk will be charted much differently when we relate to Him as such.

No one approaches God except through the Holy Spirit.

When Jesus took leave of His disciples, He assured them, *"When He, the Spirit of truth, has come, He will guide you into all truth"* (John 16:13). The original text is in Greek. Greek is a language in which the words are divided into three genders—masculine, feminine, and neuter—the corresponding pronouns of which are *he, she,* and *it.* The Greek word for *"Spirit," pneuma,* is neuter, so it would normally assume the impersonal, gender-neutral pronoun, it. This verse, however, overrides grammatical convention and uses a personal, masculine pronoun, *"He."* Why? To emphasize that the Holy Spirit is a person to whom you must relate as such. We must not relate to Him as a set of rules or as simply a doctrinal concept.

The Holy Spirit's identity as a person received further reinforcement by Jesus when He said to the disciples after His resurrection, *"Nevertheless I tell you the truth. It is to your advantage that I go away; for if I do not go away, the Helper* ["Comforter" KJV] *will not come to you; but if I depart, I will send Him to you"* (John 16:7).

This passage describes an exchange of persons. Jesus said He would return to the Father in heaven; once there, He would send the Holy Spirit, or Comforter. Just as Jesus is a person, so too the Holy Spirit, who came to take Jesus' place on earth, is a person.

This exchange is to our advantage, for Jesus said we are better off with Him in heaven and with the Holy Spirit on earth. Many people like to imagine being on earth with Jesus, watching Him teach and perform miracles. As wonderful as this would be, the Bible reveals that we can know God more intimately and come closer to Jesus through the Holy Spirit than we could by Jesus' mere physical presence on earth.

We require an advocate—someone who pleads our case before God. The Holy Spirit is the best advocate, and God sent Him to plead our case and to protect us against the devil's snares. (See Romans 8:26–27.) The Holy Spirit has an exclusive role as God's personal representative on earth.

THE
HOLY SPIRIT
IN THE CHURCH

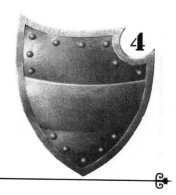

I n 2 Corinthians 3:17, Paul said, *"Now the Lord is the Spirit; and where the Spirit of the Lord is, there is liberty* [or freedom]." In the New Testament, *"Lord"* represents the sacred name of God, which is *"Jehovah"* or *"Yahweh"*; it indicates a divine person.

Paul said, *"the Lord is the Spirit."* God the Father is Lord, God the Son is Lord, and God the Spirit is also Lord. Jesus is Lord over the church, but the Holy Spirit is Lord *in* the church; Jesus' lordship over the church is effective only insofar as the Holy Spirit is Lord in the church. Should a church truly desire Jesus as Lord, the Holy Spirit must first be Lord within that church.

This requirement presents a problem to many contemporary Christian churches whose members confess Jesus as Lord but fail to make the Holy Spirit Lord in their lives and in their church meetings. They impose labels and use terms that do not authenticate the true Holy Spirit.

How does the Holy Spirit dwell within the church, the body of Christ? Paul identified two ways in his first epistle to the church at Corinth. In 1 Corinthians 3:16, he wrote, *"Do you not know that you are the temple of God and that the Spirit of God dwells in you?"* The *"you"* in this passage is plural in the original Greek; Paul was speaking to Christians collectively as a temple of the Holy Spirit.

He continued this idea in 1 Corinthians 6:19: *"Do you not know that your body is the temple of the Holy Spirit?"* Here, Paul addressed individual believers. Not only does the Holy Spirit dwell in the church—a collective group of believers—but He dwells within each individual believer. God wants to take up residence in each of us, inhabiting our physical bodies. What humility on the part of our almighty God, creator of the universe!

Why We Need the Spirit

Number of the holy Spirit

What does the Holy Spirit accomplish as He indwells us? First, He is here to complete the ministry of Jesus. Although Jesus had completed the perfect sacrifice on the cross, when He left the earth, His task of training His disciples was far from complete.

> *The Holy Spirit guides, leads, and warns of what is to come.*

Jesus had to leave them after three and a half years of companionship and instruction, but He did not abandon them. Instead, He sent the Holy Spirit to be with them forever: *"I will pray the Father, and He will give you another Helper, that He may abide with you forever"* (John 14:16). Jesus promised to send *"the Spirit of truth, whom the world cannot receive, because it neither sees Him nor knows Him; but you know Him, for He dwells with you and will be in you. I will not leave you orphans; I will come to you"* (verses 17–18).

If we attempt to live the Christian life without the Holy Spirit, we do so as orphans. Jesus provided the Holy Spirit to meet our needs, but we must welcome Him and acknowledge our dependency on Him.

Jesus again called the Holy Spirit a "Helper" in John 14:25–26:

> These things I have spoken to you while being present with you. But the Helper, the Holy Spirit, whom the Father will send in My name, He will teach you all things, and bring to your remembrance all things that I said to you.

This passage is important, for it attests that the New Testament depended not upon the apostles' memories or cleverness, but upon the Holy Spirit, who inspired their records.

Jesus never penned a word; He left to His apostles the task of recording His life and conveying His teachings in the Epistles. We can rely on the accuracy of their writings, not because they were infallible authors, but because they were authors inspired by the Holy Spirit who brought to mind Jesus' teachings. *And still is teaching me Yaay!*

The Holy Spirit completes our education as Christians. As Jesus said to the disciples in John 16:12–13,

> "I still have many things to say to you, but you cannot bear them now. However, when He, the Spirit of truth, has come, He will guide you into all truth; for He will not speak on His own authority, but whatever He hears He will speak; and He will tell you things to come."

Their distress at His departure rendered them incapable of absorbing additional teaching at the time, so further instruction by the Holy Spirit was necessary. *still*

How the Holy Spirit Helps Us

The Holy Spirit ministers to us with guidance, leading us daily. He provides us revelation, sharing with us what is to come—things spoken in heaven and manifested on earth.

Revelation is especially important during these days of increasing violence. We live in a dangerous time. All kinds of evil forces and violent acts are spreading and growing. We cannot open a newspaper without reading of crimes committed, evils perpetrated. To our advantage, however, we have someone who warns us of things to come.

God warned Noah, who by faith built an ark well before the flooding even began, in order to save his household. Jesus said that as it was in the days of Noah, so it will be in the days when He returns. (See, for example, Matthew 24:37–51.) In Noah's day, the earth was filled with violence; the thoughts of every man's heart were evil. All flesh was corrupt and perverse, engaging in immoral acts. (See Genesis 6:5.)

Only Noah was righteous before God. Because God showed him what would happen, Noah knew of the impending flood and prepared accordingly. In order to survive and fulfill our tasks as Christians in today's world, we will require a supernatural warning from God.

Distinguishing between Spirits

How can we recognize the Holy Spirit and distinguish the Holy Spirit from other spirits? There exists a counterfeit holy spirit—one example is the "holy spirit" propounded by adherents of the New Age movement.

The Holy Spirit has the distinct attribute of holiness, as indicated by His name. He is holy. In Hebrew, *Holy Spirit* is translated "the Spirit of Holiness." His other names—including the Spirit of Grace, the Spirit of Truth, and the Spirit of Power—are subsidiary to the title "Holy Spirit."

Nothing unholy proceeds from the Holy Spirit. The Scriptures speak of the beauty of holiness. (See, for example, Psalm 29:2; 96:9.) When it proceeds from the Holy Spirit, holiness gives a person an internal beauty that may or may not be mirrored externally. In 1 Peter 3:4, Peter spoke of *"the hidden person of the heart"* and *"the incorruptible beauty of a gentle and quiet spirit,"* which God values highly.

Anything ugly—in a spiritual sense—does not proceed from the Holy Spirit. Twelve key words associated with this type of ugliness should identify anything they describe as being unholy: degraded, degrading, flippant, indecent, insensitive, rude, self-assertive, self-exalting, sham, silly, stupid, vulgar. These words never apply to the Holy Spirit.

We can identify the Holy Spirit with three additional tests.

The Holy Spirit Cannot Be Manipulated

First, people who use a spirit to manipulate or dominate others practice witchcraft, for no one wields control over God's Holy Spirit. The Holy Spirit is not synonymous with the gifts of the Holy Spirit. In Romans 11:29, Paul explained that the *"gifts…of God are irrevocable."* Once God bestows a gift on someone, He never rescinds it; the recipient can use, misuse, or neglect that gift. This freedom confirms that the gift is just that—a gift, as opposed to a conditional loan.

People have long misused gifts of the Holy Spirit, as indicated by Paul in 1 Corinthians 13:1: *"Though I speak with the tongues of men and of angels, but have not love, I have become sounding brass or a clanging cymbal."* In this case, the gift of speaking in tongues—when misused—makes an empty, discordant noise.

Other spiritual gifts, such as a word of knowledge or a gift of healing, may be misused when people use them to achieve a certain end (often personal gain) or to promote a movement that opposes the will of God. Thus the Holy Spirit and His gifts are separate entities.

A gift of the Holy Spirit may be misused, but the Holy Spirit cannot be manipulated. The Holy Spirit is God, and we must relate to Him as such.

The Holy Spirit Is a Servant

A second distinguishing feature of the Holy Spirit is His role as a servant of God the Father and God the Son. This reinforces the honorable nature of servitude, something resented and rejected by many people today who miss the importance of serving. The Holy Spirit's role as a servant directs His activities and attributes. In John 16:13–14, Jesus described the Holy Spirit's ministry and activity:

When He, the Spirit of truth, has come, He will guide you into all truth; for He will not speak on His own authority, but whatever He hears He will speak; and He will tell you things to come. He will glorify Me, for He will take of what is Mine and declare it to you.

Thus, the Holy Spirit speaks no message of His own, but rather what He hears from the Father and the Son. His aim is to point to Jesus and to glorify Him. Any spirit that focuses on itself, rather than Jesus, is not the Holy Spirit.

Nowhere in Scripture have I found a prayer addressed to the Holy Spirit. What might seem an instance of prayer to the Holy Spirit—in Ezekiel's vision of the valley of barren, dry bones—is actually prophecy instead of prayer:

> *He said to me, "Prophesy to the breath, prophesy, son of man, and say to the breath, 'Thus says the Lord God: "Come from the four winds, O breath, and breathe on these slain, that they may live."'" So I prophesied as He commanded me, and breath came into them, and they lived, and stood upon their feet, an exceedingly great army.* (Ezekiel 37:9–10)

Praying to God the Father instead of to the Holy Spirit establishes a protocol based upon a master-servant relationship. When dealing with a master and his servant, you address the master directly; his servant does not act as intermediary, but rather receives instructions from the master. We never give orders to the Holy Spirit, but through prayer, we present our supplications to God the Father in Jesus' name, and God directs His servant, the Holy Spirit.

The Holy Spirit Glorifies Jesus

A third attribute of the Holy Spirit has already been mentioned in our previous point, but it is worth noting here—Jesus' statement about the Holy Spirit in John 16:14: "He [the Holy Spirit] *will glorify Me.*" Everything the Holy Spirit does glorifies Jesus. This provides a foolproof test of whether something is of the Holy Spirit: Does it glorify Jesus?

The Holy Spirit will never glorify a human personality, a doctrine, a movement, a denomination…the list could go on and on. Nothing and no one other than Jesus receives His glory. If we desire the Holy Spirit in our lives and in our worship services, the best way to attract Him is by glorifying Jesus. When we lift up Jesus—praising Him, proclaiming His victory, declaring His righteousness—this aligns us with God's will and attracts His favor and blessing.

> *Everything the Holy Spirit does glorifies Jesus.*

I recall a particular Sunday morning worship service in which the service flowed; you felt like you were on a cloud. I said to the worship leader, "That was a beautiful service this morning. Do you know why?"

Then I answered my own question: "Because Jesus was the theme all the way through, from beginning to end. That's what the Holy Spirit likes."

Note —

If we desire the Holy Spirit's anointing on our lives, in our services, and in our homes, we need to glorify Jesus—speaking about Him and worshiping Him. When we do, the Holy Spirit will gladly join the gathering.

Not only will the Holy Spirit glorify Jesus, but Jesus said the Holy Spirit also *"will take of what is Mine and declare it to you. All things that the Father has are Mine. Therefore I said that He will take of Mine and declare it to you"* (John 16:14–15). The Father has committed all He has to the Son, and everything shared by Father and Son—the sum of their wealth—is controlled by the Holy Spirit. He administers the wealth of the Godhead. To share in that wealth, we must befriend Him by glorifying Jesus.

In the British army, I was once in charge of distributing rations in a hospital. I was popular and had many friends.

Why? Because people found that by being my friend, they could obtain a little extra tea or sugar—two valuable and rare items in those days. If we want God's best, we must be friends with the Holy Spirit. He will bestow generous portions of blessings on us. *Thank for Jesus*

The Benefits of Befriending the Holy Spirit

To summarize, the benefits of befriending the Holy Spirit stem from His assignments in the church. As we have seen, some of these are teacher, reminder, guide, revelator, and administrator of wealth. *Know this*

Another assignment is to empower the body of Christ. In Acts 1:8, Jesus said, *"You shall receive power when the Holy Spirit has come upon you; and you shall be witnesses to Me in Jerusalem, and in all Judea and Samaria, and to the end of the earth."* Even though the disciples were already saved and were following Jesus, they were still powerless to complete their commission single-handedly.

After Jesus' resurrection, the disciples spent every day praising God in the temple. This was wonderful, except that the rest of Jerusa-

> *Only by the supernatural power of the Holy Spirit can we live the life God expects of us.*

lem had no idea what was happening. When the Holy Spirit came, however, it took only a few hours for everyone in Jerusalem to know something was astir. *Note* When the Holy Spirit moves, He influences people and makes an impact. He stirs people up and renders apathy impossible.

We depend upon the Holy Spirit, just as Jesus Christ did before us. In Romans 6:4, Paul said, *"Therefore we were buried*

43

with Him [Jesus] through baptism into death, that just as Christ was raised from the dead by the glory of the Father, even so we also should walk in newness of life."

The glory of the Father—the Spirit of God—raised Jesus Christ from the dead. Jesus did not raise Himself. Rather, He trusted the Father to raise Him by the Spirit. We must therefore *"walk in newness of life,"* or depend completely upon the Holy Spirit for this new walk as Christians, just as Jesus depended completely upon the Holy Spirit for His resurrection. Depend on the holy Spirit

Our own strength and wisdom will fail; neither education nor financial resources will suffice. Only by the supernatural power of the Holy Spirit can we live the type of life God expects of us. Only by the supernatural power of the Holy Spirit may we accomplish God's purpose for our lives.

The word *supernatural* makes many people uneasy, but removing all references to the supernatural in the twenty-eight chapters of the book of Acts would obliterate the book altogether. In other words, the supernatural is not strictly something from the Old Testament. New Testament Christianity—which includes today and tomorrow—also involves the supernatural. We have no hope of victory over sin without the supernatural power of the Holy Spirit. Friendship with Him helps us to cultivate true Christian character. We must speak of the Holy Spirit with respect and honor, and any blasphemy—defined as "to speak lightly or amiss of sacred things"—requires repentance. Let us make friends with the Holy Spirit today.

HUMAN PERSONALITY AND THE HOLY SPIRIT

Now may the God of peace Himself sanctify you completely; and may your whole spirit, soul, and body be preserved blameless at the coming of our Lord Jesus Christ" (1 Thessalonians 5:23). One great truth of this verse is that it contains the formula for the components of the human personality.

The Human Personality: Spirit, Soul, and Body

Most of us would agree that spirit, soul, and body constitute the complete human personality. The first chapter of Genesis says that God chose to make man in His own *"image"* and *"likeness"* (verse 26). Image refers to outward appearance; thus, something in man's outward appearance mirrors the outward appearance of God. Likeness refers to the internal structure of the triune Godhead: Father, Son, and Holy Spirit. Man's spirit, soul, and body correspond to the three components of the Trinity.

This internal structure of the human personality is traceable to God's creation of man. The human spirit proceeds from God's breath; He breathed into Adam to produce a spirit within him (see Genesis 1:7). Interestingly, in both Hebrew and Greek, the words for *spirit* and *breath* are the same. The body was clay infused with divine life to become Adam.

Proceeding from the union of spirit and body, the soul is perhaps the most difficult component to understand. It is the unique ego of each individual, the part that determines "I will" or "I won't."

Comprising will, emotions, and intellect, the soul produces statements of three corresponding types: "I want," "I think," and "I feel." These statements rule the life of natural, sinful man. When individuals surrender to these demands of their souls rather than being guided by God's Spirit, they separate themselves from God.

The Implications of Sin

Let us consider what happened to Adam and Eve because of sin. First, the spirit died, for God said to Adam in Genesis 2:17, *"But of the tree of the knowledge of good and evil you shall not eat, for in the day that you eat of it you shall surely die."* Even though Adam did not die physically for more than nine hundred years, he died spiritually the moment he disobeyed God by eating the fruit. All of Adam and Eve's offspring— all humans—are therefore rebellious by nature. When we repent, God does forgive our sins and renew our spirits.

A passage in Ephesians addresses these truths. In Ephesians 2:1–3, Paul wrote to believers who had been made alive in Christ:

> *You He made alive, who were dead in trespasses and sins, in which you once walked according to the course of this world, according to the prince of the power of the air, the spirit who now works in the sons of disobedience, among*

46

whom also we all once conducted ourselves in the lusts of our flesh, fulfilling the desires of the flesh and of the mind, and were by nature children of wrath, just as the others.

From Rebellion to Salvation

Salvation restores life to our spirits, as we read in Ephesians 2:4–6:

But God, who is rich in mercy, because of His great love with which He loved us, even when we were dead in trespasses, made us alive together with Christ (by grace you have been saved), and raised us up together, and made us sit together in the heavenly places in Christ Jesus.

God made us alive, resurrected us, and enthroned us—all in the past tense. These things have been accomplished. Spiritually, we are already seated with Christ on the throne. To reconcile our souls to God, however, we are responsible for turning from our rebellious ways through repentance. Many people who claim salvation have never renounced their rebellion.

> Surrender to the demands of the soul separates us from God.

Romans 5:1 teaches us, "*Therefore, having been justified by faith, we have peace with God through our Lord Jesus Christ.*" We were at war with God, but our faith in Christ justifies us before Him, establishing peace between us. As we read in Romans 5:11, "*Not only that, but we also rejoice in God through our Lord Jesus Christ, through whom we have now received the reconciliation.*"

While salvation cannot preserve our physical bodies, it does make them temples for the Holy Spirit to inhabit. We must treat them with reverence, as Paul exhorted in 1 Corinthians 6:19–20: *"Do you not know that your body is the temple of the Holy Spirit who is in you, whom you have from God, and you are not your own? For you were bought at a price; therefore glorify God in your body."*

When we receive salvation, our spirits are made alive, our souls are reconciled to God, and our bodies are made temples for the Holy Spirit, so that we become eligible for the first resurrection—the bodily resurrection of those who belong to God in Christ.

Functions of Spirit, Soul, and Body

Spirit

Our spirit is capable of communicating directly with God and worshiping Him, as attested by 1 Corinthians 6:17: *"He who is joined to the Lord is one spirit with Him."*

Neither soul nor body can unite with God; the spirit alone is capable of uniting with Him. And the spirit alone is capable of true worship. In John 4:23–24, Jesus said, *"But the hour is coming, and now is, when the true worshipers will worship the Father in spirit and truth; for the Father is seeking such to worship Him. God is Spirit, and those who worship Him must worship in spirit and truth."*

Soul

The soul's function is to make decisions, and regeneration enables the soul to make right decisions. In Psalm 103:1, David wrote, *"Bless the LORD, O my soul."* In this verse, his spirit is telling his soul what to do. His spirit senses the need to bless the Lord, but he requires activation by his soul to execute this need.

An everyday analogy to illustrate this concept is the gear lever in a car. You can turn the key and start the engine, but to make the car move, you must shift into drive or first gear. Similarly, the soul shifts the spirit into action.

It is often difficult to distinguish soul from spirit. The only effective dividing tool is described in Hebrews 4:12:

> For the word of God is living and powerful, and sharper than any two-edged sword, piercing even to the division of soul and spirit, and of joints and marrow, and is a discerner of the thoughts and intents of the heart.

The Word of God is the only instrument sharp enough to divide soul from spirit, and to discern their distinctions.

Two conditions to employ the Word of God in discernment are established in Hebrews 5:13–14, where the writer distinguishes between mature and immature Christians:

> For everyone who partakes only of milk is unskilled in the word of righteousness, for he is a babe. But solid food belongs to those who are of full age, that is, those who by reason of use have their senses exercised to discern both good and evil.

Discernment comes with practice and with prolonged study of the Word of God.

Distinguishing Soul from Spirit

The Greek word for spirit is *pneuma*, which means "breath," "wind," and "spirit." The corresponding adjective, *pneumatikos*, is translated as "spiritual."

The Greek word for soul is *psuche*; the corresponding adjective, *psuchikos*, means "natural," "sensual," "unspiritual," and "worldly minded." "Soulish" is a word that I created to encapsulate these meanings. Let's consider the differences between "spiritual" and "soulish" in relation to the body, as delineated in the New Testament.

Body

Paul developed the concepts of spiritual and soulish bodies in his first epistle to the Corinthians. Referring to the resurrection, he wrote, *"It is sown a natural body* [a soulish body], *it is raised a spiritual body. There is a natural* [soulish] *body, and there is a spiritual body"* (1 Corinthians 15:44).

He continues in verse 46: *"However, the spiritual is not first, but the natural* [soulish], *and afterward the spiritual."* Our present bodies are soulish; our resurrection bodies will be spiritual.

I believe this transformation will eliminate the need of a "gear lever." Our spirits will direct our bodies, determining where to go, what to say, and what to do, no longer dependent upon the soul to carry out these decisions. We will be as the cherubim described in Ezekiel 1:12: *"Each one went straight forward; they went wherever the spirit wanted to go, and they did not turn when they went."* Verse 20 says, *"Wherever the spirit wanted to go, they went, because there the spirit went."*

Decline from Earthly to Soulish to Demonic

James 3:15 is pithy yet profound: *"This wisdom does not descend from above, but is earthly, sensual, demonic."* This passage marks the steps in the decline of wisdom, a decline that allows demons to infiltrate the work, people, and church of God. Being earthly may seem innocent enough, but it takes little time for apathy to take root, dragging the individual down into the soulish realm, and perhaps further still into the realm of the demonic.

Earthly

What does it mean to be earthly? From a Christian standpoint, earthly individuals focus on our earthly life and nothing more—nothing beyond. If an earthly individual is a Christian, he expects God to provide blessings applicable only to this lifetime: prosperity, healing, power, success, and other soulish pursuits.

To gain a better understanding of the earthly individual, it is useful to recognize individuals who were decidedly unearthly. One such example is Abraham:

> *By faith he dwelt in the land of promise as in a foreign country, dwelling in tents with Isaac and Jacob, the heirs with him of the same promise; for he waited for the city which has foundations, whose builder and maker is God.*
>
> (Hebrews 11:9–10)

Abraham accepted the temporality of earthly life, dwelling in a tent instead of building a residence in the Promised Land. By contrast, Lot, who separated from Abraham and turned toward the wicked town of Sodom, lived in a house and abandoned an eternal mind-set for a mundane one.

This world is not our home. We become soulish if we forget that.

God expects us to adopt Abraham's mind-set. This world is not our home. When we forget that, we become soulish.

A second example of an unearthly individual is Moses, described in Hebrews 11:27: *"By faith he forsook Egypt, not fearing the wrath of the king; for he endured as seeing Him who is*

51

invisible." Moses endured because he looked past the present hardships to a certainty of future fulfillment.

In 1 Corinthians 15:19, Paul wrote, *"If in this life only we have hope in Christ, we are of all men the most pitiable."* If the purpose of our Christian faith is to receive blessings in this earthly life alone, we are to be pitied. Many have forgotten the fact that we are foreigners passing through this world, and consequently, their thoughts and ambitions lose proper focus. They become earthly.

Soulish

Soulish is the level below earthly. What is the essence of the soul? As described previously, the soul is essentially the ego. Soulish people are egocentric, concerned exclusively with themselves.

While the spiritual person asks, "How can I glorify God?" the soulish person asks, "What's in it for me?" The contemporary church caters too often to this quest of personal gain instead of God's glory.

In 1 Corinthians 2:14–15, Paul wrote,

But the natural [soulish] *man does not receive the things of the Spirit of God, for they are foolishness to him; nor can he know them, because they are spiritually discerned. But he who is spiritual judges all things, yet he himself is rightly judged by no one.*

The soulish man cannot discern spiritual truth because he must do so with the spirit; he is attuned solely to soulish appeals to his emotions. One can be motivated by soulishness to contribute a substantial tithe and/or offering to the church, but this improper motivation will render it ineffectual.

Soulish people worship God in order to have a good time. "Wonderful worship service," they often say. But the purpose of worship is not for us to have a good time. Rather, the purpose of worship is just what it says—worship! Proper worship praises God; it does not seek to elevate our emotions or to thrill our senses. In the process of worshipping God, our emotions may or may not be elevated or thrilled, but this should not be our primary focus.

Proper worship does not seek to elevate our emotions or thrill our senses.

Having been a preacher for many years, I have seen soulish appeals to emotion that move people to tears and make them excited—without changing them. One week later, they are usually the same. It is lamentable how many churches specialize in the realm of the soul rather than in the realm of the spirit. People in the soulish realm are carried away with little effort, setting themselves up for deception. This can be avoided only by distinguishing between the spiritual and the soulish realm.

Demonic

A step down from soulish is the demonic. The pattern of progression from earthly to soulish to demonic is perhaps best illustrated in the Old Testament by Aaron, a high priest of Israel who fashioned a golden idol. Exodus 32:1–6 describes his decline:

Now when the people saw that Moses delayed coming down from the mountain, the people gathered together to Aaron, and said to him, "Come, make us gods that shall go before us;

for as for this Moses, the man who brought us up out of the land of Egypt, we do not know what has become of him." And Aaron said to them, "Break off the golden earrings which are in the ears of your wives, your sons, and your daughters, and bring them to me." So all the people broke off the golden earrings which were in their ears, and brought them to Aaron. And he received the gold from their hand, and he fashioned it with an engraving tool, and made a molded calf. Then they said, "This is your god, O Israel, that brought you out of the land of Egypt!" So when Aaron saw it, he built an altar before it. And Aaron made a proclamation and said, "Tomorrow is a feast to the Lord [Yahweh]." Then they rose early on the next day, offered burnt offerings, and brought peace offerings; and the people sat down to eat and drink, and rose up to play.

There are several significant details in this passage to note. First, the people credited Moses for their deliverance—*"the man who brought us up out of the land of Egypt"*—instead of recognizing God's providence. Their focus on human leaders turned into idolatry.

Play is the essence of idolatry.

The passage concludes with idolatry, too—*"the people...rose up to play."* Play is the essence of idolatry, and when our worship becomes play, we have slipped from the spiritual to the soulish, and—ultimately—to the demonic.

Much of what we call "worship" in our churches is not worship at all. It is self-centered, focusing on finding out how to obtain God's healing, blessings, and other provisions. Much music in today's church services appeals to the soul, stimulating it in the same way that secular music might.

What is incredible about the backsliding of Aaron and the people is how suddenly it occurred. Two months before Aaron fashioned the golden calf, Moses received the Ten Commandments from God on Mount Sinai. The people responded appropriately with awe, fear, and reverence, as Exodus 20:18–21 describes:

Now all the people witnessed the thunderings, the lightning flashes, the sound of the trumpet, and the mountain smoking; and when the people saw it, they trembled and stood afar off. Then they said to Moses, "You speak with us, and we will hear; but let not God speak with us, lest we die." And Moses said to the people, "Do not fear; for God has come to test you, and that His fear may be before you, so that you may not sin." So the people stood afar off, but Moses drew near the thick darkness where God was.

Within two months, the people had abandoned their attitude of fear and reverence, and in its place was an attitude of indifference and idolatry. Once their physical needs had been met—their appetites sated, their bodies sufficiently clothed—they demanded entertainment in the form of worship.

A second example of slipping from the spiritual to the demonic is found in Leviticus 9:23–10:2:

Moses and Aaron went into the tabernacle of meeting, and came out and blessed the people. Then the glory of the LORD appeared to all the people, and fire came out from before the LORD and consumed the burnt offering and the fat on the altar. When all the people saw it, they shouted and fell on their faces. Then Nadab and Abihu, the sons of Aaron, each took his censer and put fire in it, put incense on it, and offered profane fire before the LORD, which He had not commanded them. So fire went out from the LORD and devoured them, and they died before the LORD.

The same fire that consumed an acceptable sacrifice consumed these men who worshiped in the wrong spirit. In our experience, *"profane fire"* is signified by worship in any spirit other than the Holy Spirit.

Restoring a Sense of Awe

In the New Testament, the book of Hebrews urges us to maintain the same awe of God that was inspired by Old Testament events, such as God's judgment on Sodom and Gomorrah. Hebrews 12:28–29 says,

Therefore, since we are receiving a kingdom which cannot be shaken, let us have grace, by which we may serve God acceptably with reverence and godly fear. For our God is a consuming fire.

A New Testament example of God's holy judgment is His striking Ananias and Sapphira dead when they cheated with their offering. *"Great fear came upon all the church and upon all who heard these things"* (Acts 5:11).

How much awe do we find in today's church?

How much awe do we find in today's church? In Britain one summer, I was talking with a minister friend who made the comment, "I meet people who talk about God as if He were someone they had met in the pub."

Many people view God as a casual friend or a close buddy. He does invite our fellowship and communion with

Him, but we must never lose a sense of awe of God's holiness. Too often, the lack of awe gives way to unscriptural frivolity and flippancy. As Charles Finney once commented, "God never uses a jester to search consciences."

One ministry of the Holy Spirit is convicting us of sin. Where conviction is lacking, the work of the Holy Spirit is most likely lacking, as well.

Avoiding Satan's Trap

The condition of humanity is not about to improve. In 2 Timothy 3:2–4, Paul warned of what humans will be like at the close of this age. He listed eighteen moral blemishes that will be prevalent:

For men will be lovers of themselves, lovers of money, boasters, proud, blasphemers, disobedient to parents, unthankful, unholy, unloving, unforgiving, slanderers, without self-control, brutal, despisers of good, traitors, headstrong, haughty, lovers of pleasure rather than lovers of God...

We notice that this list is bookended by misplaced love—love of self, love of money, and love of pleasure. Soulishness, or the love of self, lets evil in. Verse 5 concludes, "...*having a form of godliness but denying its power. And from such people turn away!*" Despite their having a form of godliness—they were probably professing Christians—the people described here indulge in self-love and the vices this invites.

Satan takes great delight in those who love and exalt themselves, for he set the precedent for this attitude. (See Isaiah 14:12–15.) He leads people astray, encouraging them to love anything—money, pleasure, power, or themselves—more than they love God. As the perversion of something meant for good, misplaced love can make us candidates for Satan's deception. He takes what is good and pure, turning it into an instrument of our own deception and demise.

In the next chapter, we will learn more about Satan's tactics so we can recognize them and avoid succumbing to them.

Satan's
Evil Agenda

Jesus will come to earth again for His bride, the church. But He is not the only one with plans for the end of this age. Satan has schemes up his sleeve to disrupt God's purposes. To resist him, we must understand what they are. These objectives describe his goals for the end of the age.

Satan rules the unregenerate, but Paul wrote to converted Christians in Ephesians 2:1–3, reminding them of their liberation:

> *You He made alive, who were dead in trespasses and sins, in which you once walked according to the course of this world, according to the prince of the power of the air, the spirit who now works in the sons of disobedience, among whom also we all once conducted ourselves in the lusts of our flesh, fulfilling the desires of the flesh and of the mind, and were by nature children of wrath, just as the others.*

Satan rules the realm God originally committed to Adam's authority. When Adam sinned and fell, he surrendered his rule of the world, turning it over to Satan. Satan's rule extends only to those disobedient to God, however; when men and women return to God with true repentance, faith, and submission, they sever Satan's legal claim over them.

The Restraining Force

Moreover, Satan's control over mankind is not unlimited. While his angel allies, who joined his rebellion, submit completely to his control, humans' submission, expressed by disobedience to God, is only partial. The Holy Spirit is the restraining influence who, by working in the hearts of men and women to effect repentance and faith in Jesus Christ, prevents Satan from taking complete control of humanity.

I believe the Holy Spirit operates through human channels to keep Satan's power in check. An early example of such a channel was Noah and his family, whom God preserved among all humanity from the flood.

Satan has two primary objectives: to gain political control on earth and to garner the worship of the world. As we approach the fulfillment of God's objectives on earth, we also come closer to the fulfillment of the goals of Satan. These goals will, however, be ultimately frustrated.

> *Satan's goals will be ultimately frustrated.*

Throughout the centuries, Satan's plans have been frustrated by the working of God's Spirit, who draws men back to God through repentance and submission. When the Spirit succeeds, Satan's dominion weakens. Left alone, the human race, which is naturally bent on sin and rebellion, would pledge complete allegiance to Satan and turn from God entirely. Thanks to the Holy Spirit, however, God's grace and mercy move in the hearts of men, directing them to repent and seek God's countenance.

Hallelujah Jesus

Satan's Supernatural Signs and Wonders

As we established before, Satan has supernatural powers at his command. The end of this age will spark a conflict of supernatural powers: God versus Satan. In 2 Timothy 3:8–9, we read about Pharaoh's sorcerers who replicated the wonders performed by Moses:

Now as Jannes and Jambres [magicians in Egypt in Moses' time] *resisted Moses, so do these also resist the truth: men of corrupt minds, disapproved concerning the faith, but they will progress no further, for their folly will be manifest to all, as theirs also was.*

At the end of the age, a clash will occur: the supernatural power of the Holy Spirit and the servants of God will battle against the supernatural power of Satan and his servants—magicians, wizards, enchanters, clairvoyants, mediums, and others who deal in the occult. Satan's servants will be put to shame, just as were the magicians in Egypt who mirrored only the first three of Moses' miracles.

Exodus 7:10 says, *"Moses and Aaron went in to Pharaoh, and they did so, just as the Lord commanded. And Aaron cast down his rod before Pharaoh and before his servants, and it became a serpent."* Pharaoh summoned his sorcerers, who succeeded in turning their rods to serpents, but the finality is significant: Aaron's rod swallowed up the sorcerers' rods. (See verses 11–12.)

Pharaoh was not fazed, however, so the conflict continued in Exodus 7:19–22:

Then the Lord spoke to Moses, "Say to Aaron, 'Take your rod and stretch out your hand over the waters of Egypt, over their streams, over their rivers, over their ponds, and over all their pools of water, that they may become blood. And there shall be blood throughout all the land of Egypt, both in buckets of wood and pitchers of stone.'" And Moses and Aaron did so, just as the LORD commanded. So he lifted up the rod and struck the waters that were in the river, in the sight of Pharaoh and in the sight of his servants. And all the waters that were in the river were turned to blood. The fish that were in the river died....Then the magicians of Egypt did so with their enchantments....

Pharaoh's magicians turned water into blood, so Pharaoh questioned why he should heed Moses' message.

The pattern continued with frogs in Exodus 8:5–6:

The LORD spoke to Moses, "Say to Aaron, 'Stretch out your hand with your rod over the streams, over the rivers, and over the ponds, and cause frogs to come up on the land of Egypt.'" So Aaron stretched out his hand over the waters of Egypt, and the frogs came up and covered the land of Egypt."

The magicians replicated the process, and Pharaoh told Moses, in effect, "I do not need to listen to you, because my magicians did everything you did." Pharaoh's heart was then hardened, and he refused to honor Moses' request.

Moses finally made an impact with his subsequent sign in Exodus 8:16–19:

The LORD said to Moses, "Say to Aaron, 'Stretch out your rod, and strike the dust of the land, so that it may become lice throughout all the land of Egypt.'" And they did so. For Aaron stretched out his hand with his rod and struck the dust of the earth, and it became lice on man and beast. All the dust of the land became lice throughout all the land of

Egypt. Now the magicians so worked with their enchantments to bring forth lice, but they could not. So there were lice on man and beast. Then the magicians said to Pharaoh, "This is the finger of God."

As in Moses' day, the final battle on earth will break out not on the plane of human reasoning and argument, but on a supernatural plane.

We Must Choose

Satan wants to distract man's attention and be worshipped. To accomplish these goals, he seeks out someone to grant him political control over the world. It was this aim that compelled him to tempt Jesus, offering power in exchange for Jesus' praise.

Satan sought to bestow power on Jesus so that those praising Jesus would, in turn, worship the source of His praiseworthiness, in this case Satan. (See Luke 4.) To this offer, Jesus responded, *"Get behind Me, Satan!"* (Luke 4:8).

Most people read this as an emphatic dismissal of Satan, but the language seems to say instead, "Follow behind Me." Jesus told Satan, "I will go first, and you may come afterward." Everywhere Christ is preached and proclaimed, the devil is permitted to follow, peddling an alternative: the false christ, or Antichrist.

Satan seeks someone to grant him political control over the world.

This presents the human race with a choice: Christ or Antichrist. It also prefigures Pontius Pilate's presenting the crowd with the choice of whom to release from prison: *"Whom do you want me to release to you? Barabbas, or Jesus who is called Christ?"* (Matthew 27:17). They chose Barabbas, the criminal, bringing about the first manifestation in human history of the spirit of antichrist. Submitting to Satan's plan, the people rejected the true Christ and chose an evil, violent man.

The end of this age will look eerily familiar: men will choose between the true Christ and false christ. First, the true Christ will be preached in all nations, accompanied by signs and demonstrations of the Holy Spirit. Next, Satan will follow, peddling the Antichrist. The decision will follow: Jesus or Barabbas? Jesus Christ or Satan?

Satan's Strategies

Because Jesus refused to bargain with him, Satan seeks another man of remarkable ability and charismatic personality to win the world's favor. In the meantime, he employs two strategies: supernatural intervention by satanic spirits and a progressive corruption of human morals and ethics. A decline in morality is already evident in the regimes of brutal rulers such as Adolf Hitler and Josef Stalin. Less obvious, but no less odious, is the use of supernatural intervention by satanic spirits. Satan will also employ false prophets and put forth false christs to deceive and destroy followers of Christ.

Intervention by Satanic Spirits

The Old Testament attests to this intervention by satanic spirits. Genesis 6:1–2 describes the time of Noah:

Now it came to pass, when men began to multiply on the face of the earth, and daughters were born to them, that the sons of God saw the daughters of men, that they were beautiful; and they took wives for themselves of all whom they chose.

I believe *"sons of God"* refers to angels—angels who rebelled against God, breached the angelic realm, and cohabited with human women. Ancient myth and historical records from many cultures confirm this event.

Verse 4 continues,

There were giants [Hebrew, *nephilim*, or "fallen ones"] *on the earth in those days, and also afterward, when the sons of God came in to the daughters of men and they bore children to them. Those were the mighty men who were of old, men of renown."*

These *"men of renown"* are called "heroes" in Greek, and in Greek mythology, most heroes trace their origins to the union between a god and a human woman, such as Zeus and Leda. Intervention from Satan and his minions spawned a lasting legacy of sin and corruption in the human race. I have known at least three women who told me that demons sought to have sexual intercourse with them.

In 1 Peter 3:19–20, we learn that Jesus preached to the spirits in Hades: *"He went and preached to the spirits in prison, who formerly were disobedient, when once the Divine longsuffering waited in the days of Noah."* The book of Jude includes a similar entry:

The angels who did not keep their proper domain [i.e., did not stay on the heavenly plane], *but left their own abode, He has reserved in everlasting chains under darkness for the judgment of the great day; as Sodom and Gomorrah, and the cities around them in a similar manner to these, having given themselves over to sexual*

*immorality and gone after strange flesh, are set forth as
an example, suffering the vengeance of eternal fire.*

(Jude 6–7)

Between His death and resurrection, Jesus descended
into Hades, where God had imprisoned spirits for specific
reasons. Greek mythology makes many references to a place
called Tartarus, the same name used in the New Testament
for the place where these imprisoned angels were cast. The
standard Greek lexicon explains that Tartarus is a place of
imprisonment, made for specific wrongdoing, located as far
below Hades as Hades is below the earth's surface. In this
respect, the Bible and Greek mythology are in accord.

Corruption and Decline in Ethics and Morals

The supernatural intervention by satanic angels was
accompanied by moral decline. Genesis 6:5 says, *"Then the
LORD saw that the wickedness of man was great in the earth, and
that every intent of the thoughts* ["every imagination" KJV] *of his
heart was only evil continually."* Men's imaginations conjured
vile notions.

Verse 11 continues, *"The earth also was corrupt before God,
and the earth was filled with violence."* Violence and bloodshed
were rife.

And verse 12 concludes, *"So God looked upon the earth,
and indeed it was corrupt; for all flesh had corrupted their way on
the earth."* Thus, prior to the flood, human degeneration was
characterized chiefly by evil thoughts, violence, and sexual
perversion.

The earliest event of God's judgment on the world, the
flood, provides a glimpse of God's final judgment, too. Again,

the Holy Spirit must work through a channel—in the case of the flood, He worked through Noah and his family.

In Genesis 7:1, God gave Noah the rationale for His choice: *"Come into the ark, you and all your household, because I have seen that you are righteous before Me in this generation."* Noah's righteousness sufficed for his family, too, a clear instance of what is declared in Acts 16:31: *"Believe on the Lord Jesus Christ, and you will be saved, you and your household."* When Noah and his family were safely withdrawn, God's Spirit withdrew from the rest of humanity, giving Satan free

The flood in Genesis provides a glimpse of God's final judgment.

reign on earth for seven days, the time when Noah and his family were sealed inside the ark before the rain came. Judgment ensued, and in the final days a similar sequence will likely transpire. Jesus said in Luke 17:26, *"As it was in the days of Noah, so it will be also in the days of the Son of Man."*

Another Wicked Ruler

Another Old Testament pattern that prefigures the end of this age occurred in the days of Ahab, a wicked ruler of the northern kingdom of Israel. His rule displayed both degeneration of human character and satanic supernatural intervention:

> *In the thirty-eighth year of Asa king of Judah, Ahab the son of Omri became king over Israel; and Ahab the son of Omri reigned over Israel in Samaria twenty-two years. Now Ahab the son of Omri did evil in the sight of the LORD, more than all who were before him. And it came to pass, as though it had been a trivial thing for him to walk in the sins*

of Jeroboam the son of Nebat, that he took as wife Jezebel the daughter of Ethbaal, king of the Sidonians; and he went and served Baal and worshiped him. Then he set up an altar for Baal in the temple of Baal, which he had built in Samaria. And Ahab made a wooden image. Ahab did more to provoke the LORD God of Israel to anger than all the kings of Israel who were before him. (1 Kings 16:29–33)

First Kings 21:25 describes Ahab's wickedness even more succinctly: *"But there was no one like Ahab who sold himself to do wickedness in the sight of the LORD, because Jezebel his wife stirred him up."* To whom did Ahab sell himself? To Satan, the author of wickedness—he made a bargain with the devil. Ahab's wife, Jezebel, prefigures the harlot, or false church. She persecuted and put to death the prophets of the Lord and promoted instead false prophets. (See 1 Kings 18:4.) Her tactics represent what we can expect from the false church at the end of the age.

False Prophets

Along with a false church, we expect false prophets and false christs to appear. Those who are not rooted in Christ and are ignorant of the power and truth of God will succumb to deception and ultimate destruction.

First Timothy 4:1 provides a clear warning: *"Now the Spirit expressly says that in latter times some will depart from the faith, giving heed to deceiving spirits and doctrines of demons."* Second Timothy 3:13 foretells, *"But evil men and impostors will grow worse and worse, deceiving and being deceived."*

Jeremiah 23:16–17 warns that false prophets speak of peace when true prophets would warn of destruction:

Thus says the LORD of hosts: "Do not listen to the words of the prophets who prophesy to you. They make you worthless; they speak a vision of their own heart, not from the mouth of the LORD. They continually say to those who despise Me, 'The LORD has said, "You shall have peace"'; and to everyone who walks according to the dictates of his own heart, they say, 'No evil shall come upon you.'"

A prophet can speak comforting words, but if we are not walking according to the truth of God, these words do not apply. The prophet fosters false comfort. Jeremiah continues, *"For who has stood in the counsel of the LORD, and has perceived and heard His word? Who has marked His word and heard it?"* (verse 18). A true prophet stands in the counsel of the Lord and turns people from evil ways.

> *Prophets turn people from their evil ways.*

False prophets cause many problems and lead astray people who look to the prophets as those who interpret God's will and God's ways. A false or fabricated interpretation leads astray those who subscribe to it. Ezekiel 22:25–27 provides a vivid example:

The conspiracy of her prophets in her midst is like a roaring lion tearing the prey....Her priests have violated My law and profaned My holy things; they have not distinguished between the holy and unholy, nor have they made known the difference between the unclean and the clean....Her princes in her midst are like wolves tearing the prey, to shed blood, to destroy people, and to get dishonest gain."

God judges prophets, priests, princes, and people, but He starts with the prophets, who represent Him and His will.

Expect an Increase

In times of spiritual decline, false prophets multiply. In the time of Elijah, late in King Ahab's reign, there were four hundred and fifty prophets of Baal and four hundred prophets of Asherah, an immoral, pagan deity. That makes eight hundred and fifty false prophets, a stark contrast to the single true prophet, Elijah.

Also during Ahab's reign, Ahab used the testimony of four hundred other false prophets to convince Jehoshaphat, King of Judah, to go to war against Ramoth-Gilead. In this instance, too, there was but one true prophet, Micaiah. This period alone witnessed twelve hundred and fifty false prophets and only two true prophets.

Do you think this stark contrast is much different today? I believe the ratio of false prophets to true prophets has changed little since then.

God's Dealings

In Ezekiel 22:23, God pronounced judgment on Israel: *"The word of the LORD came to me, saying, 'Son of man, say to her* [the land of Israel]: *"You are a land that is not cleansed or rained on in the day of indignation."'"*

When I was the principal of a college, a student named Wilson Mamboleo made a statement that has stuck with me: "The only thing that can cleanse a land is the rain of the Holy Spirit." Without the rain of the Holy Spirit, Israel was left unclean.

Ezekiel goes on to describe how God will deal with four groups: prophets, priests, princes, and people. He deals with them in this order, starting with the prophet, who interprets

God's will and God's ways to His people. Ezekiel 22:25–28 reads:

> *The conspiracy of her prophets in her midst is like a roaring lion....Her priests have violated My law and profaned My holy things; they have not distinguished between the holy and unholy, nor have they made known the difference between the unclean and the clean....Her princes in her midst are like wolves tearing the prey....Her prophets plastered them with untempered mortar, seeing false visions, and divining lies for them.*

God begins judgment with the church—with the prophets. False prophets abound, unfortunately.

> *If there arises among you a prophet or a dreamer of dreams, and he gives you a sign or a wonder, and the sign or the wonder comes to pass, of which he spoke to you, saying, "Let us go after other gods"; which you have not known; "and let us serve them," you shall not listen to the words of that prophet or that dreamer of dreams, for the LORD your God is testing you to know whether you love the LORD your God with all your heart and with all your soul. You shall walk after the LORD your God and fear Him, and keep His commandments and obey His voice; you shall serve Him and hold fast to Him.* (Deuteronomy 13:1–4)

From the above passage, we see that false prophets give predictions that may even come to pass, but they are not from God because the predictions contradict the will of God as revealed in Scripture. Deuteronomy 18:20–22 says,

> *The prophet who presumes to speak a word in My name, which I have not commanded him to speak, or who speaks in*

71

the name of other gods, that prophet shall die. And if you say in your heart, "How shall we know the word which the LORD has not spoken?"; when a prophet speaks in the name of the LORD, if the thing does not happen or come to pass, that is the thing which the LORD has not spoken; the prophet has spoken it presumptuously; you shall not be afraid of him.

We must guard against being deceived by false prophets, who either make predictions that come true but contradict the Scriptures or make predictions that do not come true, because they do not come from God. It is unscriptural to permit someone to exercise the gift of prophecy without checking what he prophesies. It must align with Scripture. *[handwritten: Always Not]*

Influx of the Occult

An influx of the occult will characterize the end of the age. Practitioners of magic, sorcery, and witchcraft will deceive themselves and others, preparing the way for the Antichrist. Wizards, magicians, clairvoyants, and other people who wield supernatural, satanic power will grow worse and worse. We saw earlier that three of the miracles Moses performed in God's name to make Pharaoh release the Israelites from Egypt were matched by the wizardry of Pharaoh's magicians, demonstrating Satan's power in the supernatural realm.

Prophecy must align with Scripture.

The wickedness of evildoers will increase, as will the goodness of the righteous, as Revelation 22:10–12 instructs:

Do not seal the words of the prophecy of this book, for the time is at hand. He who is unjust, let him be unjust still; he who is filthy, let him be filthy still; he who is righteous, let him be righteous still; he who is holy, let him be holy still.

Given such freedom, people will pursue their natural inclinations to their logical end. To the wicked, the Lord says to live it up; you don't have long. To the righteous, He says to pursue righteousness continually without being complacent.

God Will Judge Satan's Primary Target

"The time has come for judgment to begin at the house of God; and if it begins with us first, what will be the end of those who do not obey the gospel of God?" (1 Peter 4:17).

In Ezekiel 8:10–14, the prophet recorded what he witnessed in the inner court of the temple of Jehovah in Jerusalem:

I went in and saw, and there; every sort of creeping thing, abominable beasts, and all the idols of the house of Israel, portrayed all around on the walls. And there stood before them seventy men of the elders of the house of Israel, and in their midst stood Jaazaniah the son of Shaphan. Each man had a censer in his hand, and a thick cloud of incense went up. Then He said to me, "Son of man, have you seen what the elders of the house of Israel do in the dark, every man in the room of his idols? For they say, 'The LORD does not see us, the LORD has forsaken the land.'" And He said to me, "Turn again, and you will see greater abominations that they are doing." So He brought me to the door of the north gate of the LORD's house; and to my dismay, women were sitting there weeping for Tammuz.

Inside God's temple, His people were worshiping hideous demonic figures. Women wept for Tammuz, a pagan fertility god who "died" at certain seasons of the year and was thought to be resurrected in the spring.

Ezekiel 8:16 continues,

He brought me into the inner court of the LORD's house; and there, at the door of the temple of the LORD, between the porch and the altar, were about twenty-five men with their backs toward the temple of the LORD and their faces toward the east, and they were worshiping the sun toward the east.

For these abominable practices, God executes judgment on Jerusalem. He gave to those who mourned for the abominations special markings to protect them. Those without markings were destroyed. (See Ezekiel 9:4–6.)

Satan's allies are losers by default.

Satan's allies are losers by default because Satan is himself a loser. His defeat is inevitable, so if we have aligned ourselves with him, we would be smart to switch sides while we can. He will not treat us fairly or compensate us for any efforts; once he is through with us, he will spurn us. Revelation 17:16 says,

The ten horns which you saw on the beast, these will hate the harlot, make her desolate and naked, eat her flesh and burn her with fire. For God has put it into their hearts to fulfill His purpose, to be of one mind, and to give their kingdom to the beast, until the words of God are fulfilled.

Subjects of the Antichrist, the ten horns will ultimately destroy the harlot. Thus the false church will self-destruct, ruined by the same political power it manipulated to achieve its position.

The Church Today

This situation is not so foreign to the church today. In fact, I believe the same spiritual filth and abominations that infiltrated the temple in Ezekiel's day have also seeped into the professing Christian church of today.

Most noticeable of these abominations, especially among those in positions of authority, such as priests, bishops, and other clergymen, are feminism and homosexuality. Critics of the true church call it "patriarchal" and "hierarchical," attempting to overhaul its structure and practices.

Again, the person whom God will spare is he who cries and mourns for these abominations. Amos 6:3–6 illustrates this rather clearly:

Woe to you who put far off the day of doom, who cause the seat of violence to come near; who lie on beds of ivory, stretch out on your couches, eat lambs from the flock and calves from the midst of the stall; who sing idly to the sound of stringed instruments, and invent for yourselves musical instruments like David; who drink wine from bowls, and anoint yourselves with the best ointments, but are not grieved for the affliction of Joseph.

If we focus on enjoying ourselves rather than cultivating a concern for the sufferings of those around us, our spirits are far from that of Jesus.

For a more complete picture of the moral and ethical breakdown at the end of this age, we turn to 2 Timothy 3:1–5:

But know this, that in the last days perilous times will come: For men will be lovers of themselves, lovers of money, boasters, proud, blasphemers, disobedient to parents, unthankful,

75

unholy, unloving, unforgiving, slanderers, without self-con-trol, brutal, despisers of good, traitors, headstrong, haughty, lovers of pleasure rather than lovers of God, having a form of godliness but denying its power.

As the days draw to a close, we must be sure to disassociate ourselves from evil; from those who exhibit the aforementioned traits, 2 Timothy 3:5 tells us, *"Turn away!"*

We must decide with whom we will associate, for this will have great bearing on our eternal destiny. Satan plans to ensnare us. Let us resist his schemes and remain with those who follow the Lord.

MIXTURES CREATE CONFUSION AND DIVISION

A mixture of good and evil yields two main results: confusion and division. Mixed messages contain grains of truth and falsehood, giving recipients two optional responses: they can focus on the good, or true, component and accept the bad along with it; or, they can focus on the bad, or false, component, rejecting the good along with it.

In either case, God's purposes are thwarted. In the church, confusion always yields division; fault lines form according to people's focus. The recent influx in signs and wonders indicates a mixture of spirits: the Holy Spirit and unholy spirits.

Warnings against Mixtures

God warns against mixture in the Old Testament. Deuteronomy 22:9 instructs, *"You shall not sow your vineyard with different kinds of seed, lest the yield of the seed which you have sown and the fruit of your vineyard be defiled."* Furthermore, *"You shall not plow with an ox and a donkey together"* (verse 10), and *"You shall not wear a garment of different sorts, such as wool and linen mixed together"* (verse 11). God prohibits breeding mixed livestock, sowing with mixed seed, and wearing garments made of mixed material.

The principle conveyed by these prohibitions is that when you serve the Lord, you should not mix two different types of things. Sowing with mixed seed can represent a message comprised partly of truth, partly of error. Wearing a garment of mixed material is like living simultaneously in accord with Scripture and in accord with the pattern of this world. Allowing mixed livestock to breed can represent a Christian ministry group aligning itself with another group that is not Christian.

When we serve the Lord, we should not mix two different types of things.

It is useful to note that when two different species are bred, their offspring is usually sterile. For example, mating a donkey with a horse yields a mule—an animal incapable of reproducing. Christian groups that join with "mates" of a different belief system—a different breed—often yield similarly sterile results.

King Saul presents a prime example of another biblical warning against mixtures of spirits. At one time, he prophesied in the Holy Spirit; at another time, he prophesied in a demonic spirit. Despite his forty-year reign, his victories as a military commander, and his other successes, mixture proved his death knell. Just before a battle, he consulted a witch; the next day, he committed suicide on the battlefield. King Saul's mixture of spirits and the dire results should serve to discourage us from mixing spirits in our lives.

We must ask ourselves, as individuals and as a church, whether we are sowing with mixed seed. Have I combined truth and falsehood? Am I wearing a garment of mixed materials—partly the righteousness of Jesus, partly my own fleshly nature? The blessing of God will not remain on that which is a mixture of purity and impurity.

Falsehood Cloaked in Truth

Even accompanied by seeds of truth, evil is not to enter the church. We must not be passive or neutral regarding what we accept. Proverbs 8:13 instructs, *"The fear of the LORD is to hate evil."* Compromising with evil is wrong, even sinful. The devil enters via evil with a goal *"to steal, and to kill, and to destroy"* (John 10:10). This goal applies to individuals and church congregations alike, and we must take an active stance of defense against the devil's schemes. Know my Papa God word holy word

With regard to the working of God's Holy Spirit, many churches are fence-sitters—their congregations refuse to take a stance for or against, trying to reconcile God and the world, trying to keep friendly relations with both. When the Holy Spirit comes, He electrifies the fence—no more fence-sitting! We must choose one side or the other. Some churches resist the Holy Spirit to defend their neutrality, but Jesus says, in effect, *"Whoever is not with Me is against Me."* (See, for example, Matthew 12:30.)

Laxity Is Increasing

The trend today is toward permissiveness—and today's church is no exception. Possibilities seem limitless—you may find people dancing, clapping their hands, engaging in dramatic reenactments, or any previously unheard-of activities

79

in church. These may be genuine efforts to praise God, but they may also be innovations to worship that promote distraction rather than devotion.

Increasing tolerance allows increasing freedoms; few specific restrictions deter evil. God, however, objects to the laissez-faire apathy of this age. As we saw in the last chapter, 2 Timothy 3:1–5 warns,

> *But know this, that in the last days perilous times will come: For men will be lovers of themselves, lovers of money, boasters, proud, blasphemers, disobedient to parents, unthankful, unholy, unloving, unforgiving, slanderers, without self-control, brutal, despisers of good, traitors, headstrong, haughty, lovers of pleasure rather than lovers of God, having a form of godliness but denying its power.*

This forewarning of the degeneration of human character and conduct includes behaviors at which few people today even bat an eye. The above eighteen moral defects deal predominantly with misplaced love—love of self, love of money, and love of pleasure. Even people professing salvation—those *"having a form of godliness"*—are prone to exhibit these behaviors.

Barriers and Borders Are Blurring

The walls that have broken down in the church indicate fading lines of demarcation—boundaries that exist for a specific purpose of God. Based on the book of Genesis, there seem to be two boundary lines that God guards adamantly. The first of these is sexual intercourse between angels and humans, which I have already addressed in the preceding chapter. The second of these is the barrier between male and female, which nowadays has become blurred and obscured. Deuteronomy 22:5 says, *"A woman shall not wear anything that pertains to a man, nor shall a man put on a woman's garment, for all who do so are an abomination to the LORD."*

The Hebrew word for *"abomination,"* *toebah*, is the strongest word for something God detests. While this does not mean that God has preferences about fashion and clothing styles, it does mean that there must be definitive distinctions between the appearance of men and women.

God objects to the apathy of this age.

Language is becoming grievously generalized: instead of "man" or "woman," we say "person." Instead of "husband" or "wife," we say "spouse." These are two guidelines given by Microsoft in a software guide to writing, and they represent the ambiguity that God finds reprehensible.

Love Is Emphasized over Obedience

Some churches that move in unusual manifestations claim an emphasis on love. It is right to emphasize love, but not at the expense of obedience to the Lord. Any love that does not result in obedience is unscriptural. In John 14:15, Jesus instructed His disciples, *"If you love Me, keep My commandments."* First John 5:3 affirms this mandate: *"For this is the love of God, that we keep His commandments."* OBEY

Love for God is expressed in obedience. In a similar way, God's love for us relates to obedience: He chastens those He loves. As our Father, God disciplines us. In Revelation 3:19, Jesus stated, *"As many as I love, I rebuke and chasten. Therefore be zealous and repent."*

81

A British Bible teacher remarked that some Christians confuse "God is love" with its inverse, "Love is God." They assume that anything rooted in love cannot be wrong, forgetting that any love that separates people from God or produces disobedience to His Word is an illegitimate love.

Prophecies of Partial Truth

As we have seen, error can also enter the church through prophecy. Many people mistakenly think they must accept every prophecy, fearing the consequences of rejecting it. This contradicts New Testament teachings on prophecy, however. In 1 Corinthians 14:29, Paul said, *"Let two or three prophets speak, and let the others judge,"* and in 1 Thessalonians 5:19–21, he taught, *"Do not quench the Spirit. Do not despise prophecies. Test all things; hold fast what is good."* Teach me to know your will

Even though we are not to despise any manifestation of the Holy Spirit, we are indeed to test it, accepting only what is good and true. Prophets must allow others to judge them; if a prophet is not willing to be judged and tested, he should not prophesy. We must not believe prophets if they tell us, "If you judge my message, God will judge you." Rather, we must fear God's judgment if we fail to judge prophecies, for He tells us to do so. Prophets are not dictators!

> **We must use God's Word to test prophecies.**

What standard are we to use when we judge prophecies? Read Isaiah 8:19–20:

> *When they say to you, "Seek those who are mediums and wizards, who whisper and mutter," should not a people seek their God? Should they seek the dead on behalf of the living?*

82

*To the law and to the testimony! If they do not speak accord-
ing to this word, it is because there is <u>no light in them</u>.*

The ultimate test of a prophet asks, "Does he speak
according to the testimony of God's Word?" If not, there is
no light in him.

Prophecy can be misleading. In Romans 12:6, Paul wrote,
*"Having then gifts differing according to the grace that is given to
us, let us use them: if prophecy, let us prophesy in proportion to our
faith."* In other words, prophets should not exceed the measure of their faith when they prophesy.

Prophesying can prove to be an exhilarating experience,
and prophets can get carried away, even departing from
what they actually receive from the Word of God and from
the Holy Spirit.

For instance, someone may receive a true prophecy:
"There will be a great revival." But he may grow so excited
that he adds on, "And the revival will start in our church."
The first part may be true, but the second part may be false
(and vice versa). How can this happen? It occurs when a
prophet goes beyond the proportion of faith that God has
given him.

An Improper Source

A prophecy may also be accurate but not have God as its
source. Earlier we read an Old Testament warning about this
possibility. Acts 16 gives an example of a prophecy or revelation that was not from God, albeit accurate. Paul and Silas
had just arrived in the city of Philippi.

*Now it happened, as we went to prayer, that a certain
slave girl possessed with a spirit of divination met us, who*

brought her masters much profit by fortune-telling. This girl followed Paul and us, and cried out, saying, "These men are the servants of the Most High God, who proclaim to us the way of salvation." (Acts 16:16–17)

Every word this girl spoke was true. Furthermore, she was the first person in Philippi to correctly identify Paul and Silas and their role as Christ's servants. But it was not God's Spirit who was speaking through her; rather, it was a divining, fortune-telling spirit.

The passage continues, *"And this she did for many days. But Paul, greatly annoyed, turned and said to the spirit, 'I command you in the name of Jesus Christ to come out of her.' And he came out that very hour"* (verse 18). From that point on, the girl could no longer tell fortunes. It is amazing how many people practice fortune-telling—and how many times they tell the truth—but what they foresee is not from God. A lie is inevitably mixed in with the truth of their prophecies, but the truth acts as bait—if we bite it, we swallow the lie along with the truth.

I once heard about a young Christian woman who went to see a fortune-teller. The fortune-teller said to her, "You will soon be a widow. Your husband will be killed." Less than two years later, the young woman's husband was killed in a freak accident. Thereafter, the woman was racked with guilt, wondering, "Did I open the way for that to happen to my husband by going to the fortune-teller?"

Another example is more personal. At one point, I served on the pastoral staff of a church in the United States, and much of my time was spent in the ministry of deliverance. One woman approached me and said that she had been a spiritist, but she had repented and wanted deliverance. I had no foolproof evidence that she had repented, so I told her, "I am not convinced. Come back when you have really repented." She left and returned one or two weeks later, saying, "I have repented." I was still unsure about the authenticity of her repentance, but I told her, "Okay, let us pray." We prayed, and it was quite a struggle. Afterward, I needed to rest. I reclined against the speakers' platform at the front of the church, and all of a sudden, the woman said, "I see you in

Do not accept Satan's destiny for your life.

a car and it is wrecked against a tree!" Thank God I was on my guard! I proclaimed, "You divining spirit, I am not going to be in any car that will be wrecked against any tree! I do not accept that!" I believe that had I accepted this woman's vision, it indeed would have happened. This was the destiny Satan had planned for me, and just as you receive God's destiny by being open to what He says, you can receive Satan's destiny by being open to what he says. I have never wrecked a car against a tree. Had I said, "That is terrible! I am going to wreck my car," things might have turned out differently. Do not accept Satan's destiny for your life, which he may try to convince you to accept by presenting you with things you know to be true.

Final Judgment Will Separate Mixtures

A parable about the kingdom of God presented in Matthew 13 speaks of the end of this age and the coming judgment on mixtures. A farmer planted seeds of good wheat in his field. At night, an enemy sowed tares—or weeds resembling wheat—among the wheat seed. As the crop grew, the farmer's field hands found tares growing amidst the wheat. (See Matthew 13:24–30.)

This field represents Christianity, or the kingdom of God, which includes people who bear appropriate fruit—like the good wheat—and others who bear no fruit—like the tares. The servants ask the farmer whether they should uproot the tares. *"But he* [the farmer] *said, 'No, lest while you gather up the tares you also uproot the wheat with them'"* (Matthew 13:29).

We must make sure we are wheat and not tares.

This response indicates that the outward distinctions between wheat and tares were negligible; crops producing fruit were often confused with those that produced no fruit whatsoever. The farmer's response mirrors Jesus' plan for believers and nonbelievers at the end of the age: *"Let both grow together until the harvest, and at the time of harvest I will say to the reapers, 'First gather together the tares and bind them in bundles to burn them, but gather the wheat into my barn'"* (verse 30).

A key difference between this fictional farm and the kingdom of God is the discernment of the reapers. While the field hands of the farmer found it difficult to distinguish wheat from tare, God's reapers are angels, who, like God, have no problem separating true believers from false believers.

Very often, Christians who are fed up with false believers attempt to oust them from the church. God tells us to have patience, however, and to abide the presence of tares until He uproots and discards them. Our primary responsibility is to make certain of our identity as wheat rather than as tares.

When I taught students in Africa, my aim was to under-mine their objections to the gospel in order to win them to Christ. One principal objection they cited was the prevalence of hypocrites in the Christian church. Could I deny this observation? Of course not! In fact, it would be unscriptural to deny it, for the New Testament indicates that hypocrites will intermingle with true believers in the church. The pres-ence of hypocrites affirms the truth of the New Testament; just make sure you are not among them.

Standing in the Gap

In Ezekiel 22:30–31, the Lord catalogs the sins of the prophets, priests, princes, and people:

So I sought for a man among them who would make a wall, and stand in the gap before Me on behalf of the land, that I should not destroy it; but I found no one. Therefore I have poured out My indignation on them; I have consumed them with the fire of My wrath.

God sought a man to build a wall—this, I believe, con-stitutes restoration. He also sought a man to stand in the gap—to under-take intercession. A wall separates and divides, sequestering one place from another. Surrounding the con-temporary church, most dividing walls have been demolished; we must restore them, and intercessors must stand in the gap.

Intercession is a posture between God and the objects of His wrath.

Intercession is more than prayer; it is a permanent pos-ture one assumes between God and the objects of His wrath.

87

More than an occasional hour of prayer, intercession is a constant state. Abraham was a model intercessor. When the Lord planned to destroy the people of Sodom, Abraham supplicated on their behalf; he was rooted in intercessory prayer.

We must not compromise on biblical distinctions, especially because judgment will begin in the house of God. (See 1 Peter 4:17.) As God's representatives, we must portray Him faithfully and stand our ground on issues that are important to Him.

The antidote to mixture is truth—the pure, undiluted truth of God's Word. In a secular court of law, every witness must promise to speak "the truth, the whole truth, and nothing but the truth." How much more should we, as Christians, take a stand for the truth?

THE TRUE CHURCH

IS THE BRIDE OF CHRIST

Mixtures of truth and falsehood, good and evil, have started to infiltrate the church. We are likely to be confused and deceived if we fail to discern between the two opposing churches on earth today: the true church and the false church.

In 2 Corinthians 11:2, Paul explained God's intentions regarding the true church: *"For I am jealous for you with godly jealousy. For I have betrothed you to one husband* [the Lord Jesus], *that I may present you as a chaste virgin to Christ."*

This is an amazing statement, considering the types of people who composed the congregation of the church at Corinth: prostitutes, homosexuals, lesbians, drunkards, fornicators, extortionists, and others. But Paul envisioned a church made presentable as a chaste virgin to the Lord Jesus Christ through the power of Jesus' blood and God's sanctifying work. Having founded the church at Corinth, Paul claimed responsibility for betrothing the church to Christ.

Thus the concept of the church's betrothal to Jesus Christ is an apt analogy. Anyone who has made a commitment to Christ is betrothed, but not yet married, to Jesus.

Revelation 19:7 provides a beautiful picture of the imminent wedding: *"The marriage of the Lamb has come, and His wife has made herself ready."* All of heaven—the whole universe, in fact—eagerly awaits the marriage of the Lamb. God treats His bride—the true church—with love, blessings, and abundant provisions. He will share His throne with her for eternity. The concept of a betrothal between Christ and the church helps us to understand our proper relationship to Him and the church's proper attributes as His bride.

Commitment

In Paul's day, betrothal was more binding than an engagement as we know it in contemporary culture. Today, a couple may break off their engagement without catastrophic consequences. In biblical culture, however, betrothal was a sacred and solemn commitment, almost as binding as marriage but lacking consummation.

Breaking the vows of betrothal was tantamount to breaking the vows of marriage; it constituted adultery. When a woman became betrothed to a man, the marriage ceremony followed soon thereafter, joining them legally as husband and wife. The true church is totally committed to Jesus, and He to her.

Bride's Preparation and the Bestowal of Gifts

Cleansing and purification prepare the church to wed her Bridegroom, Christ. Revelation 19:8 describes the church preparing for marriage: *"To her it was granted to be arrayed in fine linen, clean and bright, for the fine linen is the righteous acts of the saints."* She will be adorned with jewels—the gifts of the Holy Spirit. Paul wrote in his first epistle to the Corinthians,

I thank my God always concerning you for the grace of God which was given to you by Christ Jesus, that you were enriched in every thing by Him in all utterance and all knowledge, even as the testimony of Christ was confirmed in you, so that you come short in no gift, eagerly waiting for the revelation of our Lord Jesus Christ, who will also confirm you to the end, that you may be blameless in the day of our Lord Jesus Christ. (1 Corinthians 1:4–8)

When a man proposes marriage to a woman, he typically gives her a beautiful diamond ring. Can you imagine a woman agreeing to marriage but rejecting the ring? This response would render the prospect of marriage unlikely.

In the same way, the church that rejects Jesus' endowment of spiritual gifts will probably not become His bride. She needs to accept His gifts, being fully equipped and beautifully adorned for her wedding day. Isaiah 61:10 praises God for His adorning work:

I will greatly rejoice in the LORD, my soul shall be joyful in my God; for He has clothed me with the garments of salvation, He has covered me with the robe of righteousness, as a bridegroom decks himself with ornaments, and as a bride adorns herself with her jewels.

Although some Christians have donned the garments of salvation, they have yet to put on the robe of righteousness. When Jesus saves us, He covers us with this very robe; if this prospect does not excite us as an engagement ring would a young bride, there may be something amiss.

Again, the church prepares herself, *"arrayed in fine linen, clean and bright, for the fine linen is the righteous acts of the saints"*

.velation 19:8). The wedding garment is woven of many linen threads that represent the righteous acts we have performed; if that is so, a great number of righteous acts will be necessary to make an entire gown. I sometimes wonder whether some of us will have enough material to weave such a garment. Some of us may be scantily clad; anticipating the wedding day makes us hasten to fashion a wedding gown that will cover us fully.

> *Christ will appear to those who eagerly await Him.*

Anticipation

Another characteristic of the church as bride should be an eager anticipation of her Bridegroom's arrival. Hebrews 9:28 says, *"Christ was offered once to bear the sins of many. To those who eagerly wait for Him He will appear a second time, apart from sin, for salvation."* The true church is excited about the return of Christ. He will appear to those who eagerly await Him. Can you imagine a bride twiddling her thumbs or yawning when she hears that her bridegroom is on his way?

A friend of mine who is a preacher once remarked that when Jesus returns, He will expect the church to say something more than simply, "Nice to have You back." Titus 2:12–13 tells us that we should *"live soberly, righteously, and godly in the present age, looking for the blessed hope and glorious appearing of our great God and Savior Jesus Christ."*

Submission

As Christians, we must commit fully to the true church, submitting to Christ, her Bridegroom. The relationship is

92

modeled by Paul in Ephesians 5:22–23: *"Wives, submit to your own husbands, as to the Lord. For the husband is head of the wife, as also Christ is head of the church; and He is the Savior of the body."*

Christ is Head of the church, and His relationship to her is the same as a husband to his wife. As a faithful wife relates to her husband, so must the church relate to her husband, Jesus Christ. This relationship is characterized by love, honor, submission, faithfulness, and loving service. A wife submits to her husband; the church submits to Christ.

In Ephesians 5:25–27, Paul continued,

Husbands, love your wives, just as Christ also loved the church and gave Himself for her, that He might sanctify and cleanse her with the washing of water by the word, that He might present her to Himself a glorious church, not having spot or wrinkle or any such thing, but that she should be holy and without blemish.

When the church submits to God, it overflows with His glory and becomes beautiful. God will bring holiness to His church with the cleansing waters of His Word.

The Greek language has two terms for "word": *logos,* meaning the written word, and *rhema,* meaning a spoken word. Faith results from hearing the *rhema,* and so the preaching and teaching of God's Word will cleanse His church.

Christ Is the Head of the Church

In Ephesians 4:15–16, Paul used an anatomical analogy to describe our relationship to Christ:

Speaking the truth in love, [we] may grow up in all things into Him who is the head; Christ; from whom the whole

Written – logos

spoken – Rhema

body, joined and knit together by what every joint supplies, according to the effective working by which every part does its share, causes growth of the body for the edifying of itself in love.

The whole body depends on the head, by which it obtains instruction to grow, find nourishment, and function effectively. The same is true of the body of Christ, a fellowship that comprises all believers. An impaired relationship to the Head deprives the body of Christ of life-giving spiritual nourishment and direction. Deception impairs this relationship. Paul warned believers about this in Colossians 2:18–19:

Let no one cheat you of your reward, taking delight in false humility and worship of angels, intruding into those things which he has not seen, vainly puffed up by his fleshly mind, and not holding fast to the Head, from whom all the body, nourished and knit together by joints and ligaments, grows with the increase that is from God.

When we sever connection with the Head, we fall into error, deception, or false teaching that contradicts the truth of God. Believers can avoid these dangers by maintaining a right relationship to Jesus Christ, the Head. Let no one interfere with your personal connection to Him.

Four Primary Functions of the Head

Jesus Christ as our Head has four primary functions that can be understood in light of the functions of a head as it relates to the body.

1) First, a head receives input, both from the external environment via the five senses, and from internal systems,

94

such as organs and cells that communicate with nerve receptors in the brain. God hears us—He knows our thoughts, our needs, and our longings. *Thank you Papa God*

2) Second, the head makes decisions, telling the body what to do. The head has sole decision-making capabilities. In John 15:16, Jesus told His apostles, *"You did not choose Me, but I chose you."* God chose to save you; the initiative to redeem the people of the world proceeds not from the world or its inhabitants, but from God. He chooses those of us who will bear enduring fruit, as Jesus elaborated in John 15:16: *"I...appointed you that you should go and bear fruit, and that your fruit should remain, that whatever you ask the Father in My name He may give you."*

> *The initiative to redeem the people of the world proceeds from God.*

3) Third, the head initiates action. The body's intentional muscular movement responds to stimuli sent by the brain. You may establish any number of religious programs in the church, but if God did not initiate them, they will bear no fruit whatsoever, much less lasting fruit.

4) Fourth, the head coordinates the activity of the body parts, which carry out the decisions it makes.

Implications in the Christian Life

God's choice is crucial to our lives as Christians, and I believe God is involved in our lives to the degree that He has ordained what we are to pursue. Take marriage, for example. If you consider marrying, I advise you to marry the person God chooses. Do not decide for yourself.

I have been twice married; both wives have since gone home to be with the Lord. My first marriage lasted thirty years; my second, twenty years. Both marriages proved to be happy and successful, but only because God arranged them. I have never chosen a wife. God knew I was not intelligent enough to make the right choice, so He intervened and directed my path.

Seeking God's Choice

Let us consider an example in which Jesus' disciples asked for God's guidance concerning a crucial ministry matter. Just before the day of Pentecost, the eleven apostles assembled in Jerusalem. One of the original apostles was missing, though—Judas Iscariot—and there had to be twelve apostles, just as there will be twelve foundations and twelve gates in the wall of the New Jerusalem. (See Revelation 21:12, 14.)

Peter, the leader, knew that one was missing, so he said,

Therefore, of these men who have accompanied us all the time that the Lord Jesus went in and out among us, beginning from the baptism of John to that day when He was taken up from us, one of these must become a witness with us of His resurrection. (Acts 1:21–22)

Peter established specific qualifications for the twelfth apostle: he had to have been present throughout the ministry of Jesus, and he had to have witnessed Jesus from His resurrection until His ascension.

Two men met these qualifications: *"Joseph called Barsabas, who was surnamed Justus, and Matthias"* (Acts 1:23). At this point, the apostles drew lots; their own understanding could take them no further. Desiring God's choice, they could do nothing but draw lots, toss a coin, or organize another "random," objective way to allow God's choice to manifest itself. Acts 1:24–26 says,

> They prayed and said, "You, O Lord, who know the hearts of all, show which of these two You have chosen to take part in this ministry...." And they cast their lots, and the lot fell on Matthias. And he was numbered with the eleven apostles.

Matthias was God's choice as the twelfth apostle. God's choice expresses His initiative, and God's initiative expresses His headship. The church must repent of being presumptuous, for by exerting our own initiative we deny Jesus' headship.

Believers likewise sought God's choice in Acts 13:1–3:

> Now in the church that was at Antioch there were certain prophets and teachers: Barnabas, Simeon who was called Niger, Lucius of Cyrene, Manaen who had been brought up with Herod the tetrarch, and Saul. As they ministered to the Lord and fasted, the Holy Spirit said, "Now separate to Me Barnabas and Saul for the work to which I have called them."

While they awaited the Lord's decision, these prophets and teachers fasted and worshiped. How often does the church approach God with its own agenda instead of asking Him, "What is Your agenda?" God is not there just to dispense rubber stamps of approval on our ideas.

These men were apostles not of their own will but of God's, for an apostle is "one who is sent forth." The act of sending forth implies a sender; in this case, God commissioned their ministry and sent them out. It is interesting to note, however, that although the initiative proceeded from

God the Father by Jesus Christ the Son and through the Holy Spirit, these men were not called apostles before the church had sent them out. God does not bypass the church in appointing ministries.

Serving and Waiting

In 1 Thessalonians 1:9–10, Paul wrote to some of the earliest Christians about the impact of the gospel in Thessalonica: *"They themselves declare concerning us what manner of entry we had to you, and how you turned to God from idols to serve the living and true God, and to wait for His Son from heaven."* The Christians were responsible to both serve and wait.

Waiting affirms your trust in God's providence.

These two functions define the totality of the Christian life. Serving is not all of it; serving should also be accompanied by waiting, or being still. (See Psalm 46:10.)

The Bible makes more than fifty references to the necessity of waiting on God or for God. The New International Version of the Bible provides a vivid translation of Isaiah 64:4: *"Since ancient times no one has heard, no ear has perceived, no eye has seen any God besides you, who acts on behalf of those who wait for him."* God acts on behalf of those who wait on Him. Waiting is a mark of faith; it affirms your trust in God's providence. Waiting also acknowledges our dependence upon God.

I have a strong conviction that the church will not progress beyond its position today until it learns to wait on God. I believe Jesus will come back to a church that awaits Him, and that in God's providence, a period of time will come when we will cease to serve and simply will wait. The serving will be complete; all that will remain will be to wait.

THE FALSE CHURCH IS
THE BRIDE OF THE ANTICHRIST

A s I previously established, a false church will emerge from the true church, leading some believers astray as part of Satan's agenda for the end of the age. When did the church's cord first split into true and false strands? We must plumb the origins of Christianity—and the origins of human history—to discover the answer.

Origins and Attributes of the False Church

The split between the false church and the true church actually began with Adam and Eve's two sons, Cain and Abel. Genesis 4:3–5 reads,

> *In the process of time it came to pass that Cain brought an offering of the fruit of the ground to the LORD. Abel also brought of the firstborn of his flock and of their fat. And the LORD respected Abel and his offering, but He did not respect Cain and his offering.*

Abel brought before God an acceptable sacrifice, and God was pleased; Cain brought an unacceptable sacrifice and resented God's disapproval. (See verses 5–7.) Let us consider the differences between these brothers and their sacrifices,

God was pleased with Abel
Not his brother cain

for every individual is either a follower of Abel—the true church—or Cain—the false church.

First of all, Abel received a divine revelation, as indicated

Every individual follows either the true church or the false church.

by Hebrews 11:4: *"By faith Abel offered to God a more excellent sacrifice than Cain."* His faith evidences a divine revelation, for Romans 10:17 says faith comes by hearing the word of God. Somehow Abel knew that God commanded a living sacrifice be offered on the altar. By his sacrifice, Abel acknowledged the need for a sacrificial substitute to cleanse his sin. Cain, on the other hand, rejected the requirements given through divine revelation and gave something other than a living sacrifice. Abel's sacrifice offered propitiation for the curse God put upon the ground in Genesis 3:17–18 after Adam and Eve disobeyed Him; Cain's sacrifice did nothing to revoke the curse, so his sacrifice was rejected. Abel's faith produced a martyr; Cain's lack of faith, a murderer. (See Genesis 4:8–12.) This contrast alone manifests the difference between them.

Abel's kind of faith produces the true church, which is the bride of Christ; Cain's lack of faith produces the false church, which is the prostitute and harlot church. Revelation 17:6 says, *"I saw the woman, drunk with the blood of the saints and with the blood of the martyrs of Jesus. And when I saw her, I marveled with great amazement."*

Cain was a murderer; Abel, a martyr. The false church murders the righteous martyrs. These opposing attributes characterize the false church and the true church.

The False Church Began in the Old Testament

The false church is equated with Babylon of Old Testament history. This is indicated in Revelation 17:5: *"On her forehead a name was written: Mystery, Babylon the Great, the Mother of Harlots and of the Abominations of the Earth."* Babylon had several distinctive features that parallel features of the false church. First, Babylon persecuted the true people of God and destroyed the kingdom of Judah.

Second, it practiced idolatry and the occult. Isaiah 47:12–13 speaks of these practices:

> *Stand now with your enchantments and the multitude of your sorceries, in which you have labored from your youth.... You are wearied in the multitude of your counsels; let now the astrologers, the stargazers, and the monthly prognosticators stand up and save you from what shall come upon you.*

Jeremiah 50:38 also speaks of Babylon's idolatry: *"A drought is against her waters, and they will be dried up. For it is the land of carved images, and they are insane with their idols."* An idol is anything that we put first in our lives besides God or consider more important than He. Babylon was the capital city of idolatry and the occult in ancient times, and the false church is a spiritual Babylon.

Revelation 17:2 further describes the false church, *"with whom the kings of the earth committed fornication, and the inhabitants of the earth were made drunk with the wine of her fornication."* Chapter 18 adds that *"the kings of the earth have committed fornication with her, and the merchants of the earth have become rich through the abundance of her luxury"* (verse 3). Fornication in this case means false religion, or idolatry. False teachings lead followers—the kings and wealthy merchants—into this fornication.

The False Church Exploits Political Power

Looking more closely at Cain's church—the harlot—one sees first that it exploits political power. From the time the Roman Emperor Constantine made *The church is not called to run the political system.* Christianity the official religion of the empire in the fourth century, Christianity has been in decline. In the Middle Ages, the pope wielded two swords— one religious, another political—and the church experienced a backsliding. The church is not called to run the political system. Rather, we are called to pray for our political leaders and to serve in the civic sphere when called upon by God.

Revelation 13:1 describes a political federation portrayed as a beast: *"I saw a beast rising up out of the sea, having seven heads and ten horns, and on his horns ten crowns, and on his heads a blasphemous name."* Revelation 17:3 paints a picture of the false church, or harlot:

> He [one of the seven angels] *carried me away in the Spirit into the wilderness. And I saw a woman* [the false church] *sitting on a scarlet beast which was full of names of blasphemy, having seven heads and ten horns.*

This illustration clearly shows the harlot—the false church—riding to power atop the beast—the political system.

In Revelation 17:12–13, the angel explained,

The ten horns which you saw are ten kings who have received no kingdom as yet, but they receive authority for one hour as kings with the beast. These are of one mind, and they will give their power and authority to the beast.

In the end, the beast commits itself into the authority of the Antichrist.

Just as the true church is the bride of Christ, the false church is the bride of the Antichrist. The false church serves Satan, giving him all she has, and he treats her as he does anyone who submits to him: he squeezes her like a lemon, extracting all the juice and discarding the peel.

The False Church Targets the Wealthy

As it seeks to gain political power and to manipulate world leaders, the false church aims its efforts primarily at the wealthy. This should arouse our suspicion, as should any group or movement aimed specifically at the affluent.

Jesus said the gospel is preached to the poor (see, for example, Matthew 11:5), and although this does not exclude the wealthy, where they are the sole audience, the message is probably not motivated by the Holy Spirit.

Wealth has long drawn people from true belief and into false religion or idolatry. Revelation 17:4 reads, "*The woman* [the false church] *was arrayed in purple and scarlet, and adorned with gold and precious stones and pearls, having in her hand a golden cup full of abominations and the filthiness of her fornication.*" With her "*golden cup*" of lavish wealth and ostentatious extravagance, the false church has seduced multitudes and has drawn them away from the truth.

The false church's appeal is to the soul, not to the spirit. Revelation 18:11–13 gives a more detailed description of the false church's alluring lavishness:

And the merchants of the earth will weep and mourn over her [at her destruction], *for no one buys their merchandise anymore: merchandise of gold and silver, precious stones and pearls, fine linen and purple, silk and scarlet, every kind of citron wood, every kind of object of ivory, every kind of object of most precious wood, bronze, iron, and marble; and cinnamon and incense, fragrant oil and frankincense, wine and oil, fine flour and wheat, cattle and sheep, horses and chariots, and bodies and souls of men.*

The False Church Is a Harlot, an Unfaithful Bride

Again, the concept of betrothal provides a fitting illustration of the divergence of the false church from the true church. While the true church remains faithful to her vows of betrothal, the false church is unfaithful, breaking her vows and becoming a prostitute, an immoral harlot.

> *The false church appeals to the soul, not the spirit.*

Paul explained how Christians come to break their commitment to Christ: *"But I fear, lest somehow, as the serpent deceived Eve by his craftiness, so your minds may be corrupted from the simplicity that is in Christ"* (2 Corinthians 11:3). Believers break off their betrothal when their minds are corrupted.

Corruption often comes when the gospel's simplicity is complicated and misapplied. The gospel message is simple. It contains historical facts stated succinctly in 1 Corinthians

Jesus I need you I love you for Jesus)

15:3–4: *"Christ died for our sins according to the Scriptures, and that He was buried, and that He rose again the third day according to the Scriptures."*

The essential truths of the gospel are simple enough for a six-year-old to understand them; a six-year-old can often understand better than a twenty- or thirty-year-old can. Be wary when people invoke psychiatrists, philosophers, or scientists to endorse the Bible's validity; unlike other religions, such as Buddhism, Hinduism, and Islam, Christianity is tied to human history.

> *Believers break off their betrothal to Christ when their minds are corrupted.*

The false church is ushered in by false teachers, such as those who came to various churches after Paul had ministered there, and who added legal restrictions and complex elements to the gospel. Paul warned about these teachers in 2 Corinthians 11:4, saying,

For if he who comes preaches another Jesus whom we have not preached, or if you receive a different spirit which you have not received, or a different gospel which you have not accepted; you may well put up with it!

The progression of these phrases—*"another Jesus," "a different spirit,"* and *"a different gospel"*—is significant. They center on Jesus, who said, *"I am...the truth"* (John 14:6). When you alter attributes of Jesus and present a historically inaccurate picture of Christ, you create a different spirit that results in another gospel.

Paul admonished the Galatians,

I marvel that you are turning away so soon from Him who called you in the grace of Christ, to a different gospel, which is not another; but there are some who trouble you and want to pervert the gospel of Christ. But even if we, or an angel from heaven, preach any other gospel to you than what we have preached to you, let him be accursed. (Galatians 1:6–8)

The word "accursed" comes from a Greek word we also use in English, *anathema.* There is no stronger word to describe that which God completely condemns and rejects. If we receive a gospel other than the gospel of the New Testament, we are accursed unless we repent.

The False Church Follows a False Version of Jesus

Three false versions of Jesus seem to prevail today. The first casts Him as a sort of oriental guru. The New Age movement, in particular, views Jesus in this way.

The second version of Jesus, promoted especially in South America, casts Him as a Marxist revolutionary. This view, known as Liberation Theology, teaches that Christians chiefly must feed the poor, eliminate the wealthy, demand social justice, and establish a new political order, forgetting that Jesus never made any of these things His chief priority.

> *Jesus never sought to use force to establish a new social order.*

Despite His great compassion for the poor and unfortunate, Jesus never sought to use force to establish a new social order. When He was arrested after Judas' betrayal, Jesus said, *"My kingdom* is not of this world. If My kingdom were of this world, My servants would fight" (John 18:36). Demanding social justice and political change in the name of Jesus contradicts scriptural teaching.

The third false version of Jesus is that of a universal Father Christmas: a jolly, benign fellow who walks around patting people on the head and saying, "There, there; never mind. It will all work out; don't worry." This false picture of Jesus is

Demanding social justice in Jesus' name is unscriptural.

purveyed by liberal churches, where God's judgment of sin is scarcely mentioned.

Recognizing the False Church

First Timothy 4:1 warns of deception at the close of this age: *"Now the Spirit* [the Holy Spirit] *expressly says that in latter times some will depart from the faith, giving heed to deceiving spirits and doctrines of demons."* You cannot depart from the faith if you were never in the faith, so this passage is particularly sobering. It says that people who have believed the gospel and received Jesus Christ will go astray, following deceptive demons and false teaching. Stay in Jesus don't stray

False teachings will hinder the spread of the true gospel, and where the true gospel is preached, *"they will deliver you up to tribulation and kill you, and you will be hated by all nations for My name's sake. And then many will be offended, will betray one another, and will hate one another"* (Matthew 24:9–10). This effect has long been a reality. Jesus counseled, *"Then many false prophets will rise up and deceive many. And because lawlessness will abound, the love of many will grow cold. But he who endures to the end shall be saved"* (verses 11–13).

107

Holy spirit J love you in Jesus name
Papa God thank you for my love
for me

As Christians, we are promised persecution, betrayal, opposition, the rise of deception, and lawlessness. If you endure all this, you will be saved. This statement does not invalidate your salvation if you have secured it, but it means that to stay saved, you must endure.

To stay saved, you must endure.

What will indicate when this age is coming to an end? Matthew 24:14 provides the answer: *"This gospel of the kingdom will be preached in all the world as a witness to all the nations, and then the end will come."* In the face of mounting opposition and risk, the good news will spread throughout the world and a special breed of Christians will outlast the opposition. They will resist the false church.

Coming Judgment on the False Church

Neither Babylon nor the false church will escape God's judgment. Revelation 18:8–10 foretells coming retribution:

Therefore her plagues will come in one day; death and mourning and famine. And she will be utterly burned with fire, for strong is the Lord God who judges her. The kings of the earth who committed fornication and lived luxuriously with her will weep and lament for her, when they see the smoke of her burning, standing at a distance for fear of her torment, saying, "Alas, alas, that great city Babylon, that mighty city! For in one hour your judgment has come."

God will judge the false church in a swift act of finality and totality. Christians must discern the true church from the false church in order to separate themselves from the false church and the wrath she will incur, as Revelation 18:4

108

says: *"I heard another voice from heaven saying, 'Come out of her, my people, lest you share in her sins, and lest you receive of her plagues.'"* We must disassociate ourselves from this false religious system.

Second Timothy speaks in great detail about the necessity of separating ourselves from evildoers:

> *Nevertheless the solid foundation of God stands, having this seal: "The Lord knows those who are His," and, "Let everyone who names the name of Christ depart from iniquity." But in a great house there are not only vessels of gold and silver, but also of wood and clay, some for honor and some for dishonor.* (2 Timothy 2:19–20)

A "great house" such as the church contains vessels for honor and dishonor. Which type will we be? If we aspire to be vessels for honor, we must heed this passage:

> *Therefore if anyone cleanses himself from the latter [vessels for dishonor], he will be a vessel for honor, sanctified and useful for the Master, prepared for every good work. Flee also youthful lusts; but pursue righteousness, faith, love, peace with those who call on the Lord out of a pure heart.* (verses 21–22)

If we desire to follow righteousness, faith, peace, and love, we must be with those who call on the Lord from a pure heart. Yes

10

RECOGNIZE
AND RESIST
THE ANTICHRIST

T he true church is the bride of the true Christ; the false church is wed to the false christ, or the Antichrist. The Old Testament word for Christ is "Messiah" (Daniel 9:25–26)—*Mashiach*, in Hebrew. Not only is there the true Messiah, Jesus Christ, but false messiahs exist as well.

A warning for believers appears in 1 John 2:18: *"Little children, it is the last hour [the last period of this age]; and as you have heard that the Antichrist is coming, even now many antichrists have come, by which we know that it is the last hour."* The word *"antichrist"* comprises two parts—*Christ*, which we just discussed, and *anti*, which in Greek means both "against" and "in place of." These meanings describe the aim of the Antichrist: to oppose the true Christ and to usurp His place. At the end of this age, many antichrists will appear and work to oppose Christ, seeking to replace Him.

Note   Human rebellion will reach its peak before the Antichrist arrives; as Daniel 8:23 records, *"In the latter time of their kingdom, when the transgressors have reached their fullness, a king shall arise, having fierce features, who understands sinister schemes."*

Watch you do not be decieved

111

Most Bible commentators concur that the Antichrist is identical to this *"King,"* a king who will come once the rebels have reached the extreme.

Features of the Antichrist

The end of the age, therefore, will usher in the Antichrist—a specific, evil individual—as well as many antichrists, false spirits, and false prophets. False prophets speak with false spirits—spirits that deny Jesus' identity as Messiah. We are directed by 1 John 4:1 to test the spirits to know *False doctrines deny that Jesus came in the flesh.* which prophecies and revelations to believe. Verse 2 explains, *"By this you know the Spirit of God: Every spirit that confesses that Jesus Christ has come in the flesh is of God."* If a doctrine does not acknowledge that Jesus the Messiah has come in the flesh, that constitutes a false doctrine. Verse 3 continues, *"Every spirit that does not confess that Jesus Christ has come in the flesh is not of God. And this is the spirit of the Antichrist, which you have heard was coming, and is now already in the world."*

The Antichrists Will Originate in the Church

What distinctive marks will characterize the spirit of antichrist, which will accompany the Antichrist and win people to his side? One answer is found in 1 John 2:19:

> They [antichrists] *went out from us, but they were not of us; for if they had been of us, they would have continued with us; but they went out that they might be made manifest, that none of them were of us.*

112

This passage indicates that a distinctive mark of the spirit of antichrist is that it originates with the backslidden people of God. It cannot originate in paganism—which worships idols and false gods—because opposing God necessitates knowing about Him, and pagan religions are by definition ignorant of God.

The spirit of antichrist can operate only where Christ has been proclaimed. This spirit is Satan's last hope, his final attempt to foil God's purposes.

The Antichrist Denies the Messiah

The second indicator of the spirit of antichrist appears in 1 John 2:22: *"Who is a liar but he who denies that Jesus is the Christ* [Messiah]*?"* The spirit of antichrist, while aware of Jesus' coming, denies His claim to be Messiah. The above verse also includes the third indicator: *"He is antichrist who denies the Father and the Son."* The spirit of antichrist rejects the biblically revealed persons of the Godhead: Father and Son.

The Antichrist Leads People to Apostasy

Paul gave further insights about the Antichrist and the end of this age in 2 Thessalonians 2:1–4:

Now, brethren, concerning the coming of our Lord Jesus Christ and our gathering together to Him, we ask you, not to be soon shaken in mind or troubled, either by spirit or by word or by letter, as if from us, as though the day of Christ had come. Let no one deceive you by any means; for that Day will not come unless the falling away comes first, and the man of sin is revealed, the son of perdition, who opposes and exalts himself above all that is called God or that is worshiped, so that he sits as God in the temple of God, showing himself that he is God.

In Paul's day, people were already talking about the day of the Lord, so heed the Scriptures and do not believe people who tell you that the day of the Lord has come. The day of the Lord will not arrive, Paul said, until *"the falling away,"* or the apostasy. This means a deliberate rejection of revealed truth. Clearly, this apostasy must occur where truth has already been revealed: in the church.

The day of the Lord will not arrive until the apostasy.

I believe the apostasy has already begun. The church seems to have started backsliding from the basic truths of the Christian faith affirmed by the Apostles' Creed: that Jesus is the Son of God, that He was conceived of a virgin, that He led a sinless life, that He died an atoning death, that He was buried and raised again from the dead three days later, and that He will come again in power and glory to judge the living and the dead alike.

Throughout the centuries, the church has affirmed these central tenets. But in the past few decades, leaders in the professing church have publicly reneged on these truths. For example, I have the impression that many pastors, priests, and other church leaders do not believe that Jesus was physically resurrected from the dead. Even churches that do not publicly deny canonized truth may have leaders who harbor secret skepticism amounting to apostasy.

Other churches and religions take an increasingly relativistic approach, advocating a universal religion that incorporates components of every religion. Some people favor combining the three monotheistic religions—Christianity, Islam, and Judaism. This would be convenient, except for the fact that Jesus said, *"I am the way, the truth, and the life. No one comes to the Father except through Me"* (John 14:6). This claim—that Jesus is the exclusive way to salvation—offends many people today. *Thank you my Jesus I love you.*

Wild Beast versus Lamb of God

The Antichrist is known by three additional titles: *"man of sin," "son of perdition,"* and *"beast."* In the New Testament, *"son of perdition"* also refers to Judas Iscariot, the disciple of Jesus who betrayed Him. (See John 17:12.) Synonymous with *"man of sin,"* the *New King James Version* calls the Antichrist *"lawless one."* (See 2 Thessalonians 2:8–9.)

The book of Revelation makes a deliberate contrast between the beast and the Lamb. The world must choose between the two, a choice reminiscent of one whose consequences were eternally decisive: when Pilate invited the crowd to choose Jesus or Barabbas for release. Presented with Jesus, the peaceful Lamb, and Barabbas, the violent criminal, the people chose Barabbas. And history will repeat itself. Confronted with a choice between Jesus the Lamb and the Antichrist (the beast), the vast majority of the human race will choose the beast.

I choose JESUS

A lamb represents purity, meekness, and a life laid down.

The antithesis of a beast, a lamb represents purity, meekness, and a life laid down. If we want to cultivate the "Lamb nature" within, modeling ourselves after Jesus' example, we must be prepared to suffer, to lay down our lives. If we are not prepared to do so—if we have selfish, soulish things at heart—we model ourselves after the beast.

In John 5:43, Jesus spoke to the Jews, saying, *"I have come in My Father's name, and you do not receive Me; if another comes in his own name, him you will receive."* The Jewish encyclopedia records at least forty false messiahs who have emerged since the time of Jesus and who have attracted significant followings among Jewish people. These include Bar Kochba, who led the last revolt against Rome in the first century A.D., and Moses of Crete, who led several thousand followers into the ocean, convinced they would meet the messiah—they all perished. In the seventeenth century, Sabbatai Zevi claimed to be the messiah and led a movement of Jews back to their homeland. When his quest failed, he converted to Islam.

> *We must be prepared to suffer and lay down our lives.*

Thus, Jesus' prophecy has already been fulfilled, is being fulfilled, and will continue to be fulfilled: until He returns, people will accept false christs who come in their own names.

The Mark of the Antichrist

The book of Revelation foretells that when the Antichrist comes, he will establish a regime through which he will dominate humanity:

He causes all, both small and great, rich and poor, free and slave, to receive a mark on their right hand or on their foreheads, and that no one may buy or sell except one who has

*the mark or the name of the beast, or the number of his
name. Here is wisdom. Let him who has understanding
calculate the number of the beast, for it is the number of a
man: his number is 666.*   (Revelation 13:16–18)

This regime will privilege those who submit to the Antichrist by giving them sole access to life's necessities; those without a mark to prove submission will be prohibited from shopping, purchasing food, and obtaining other staples.

Those who submit to the Antichrist will be identified by one of three things: a mark, his name, or his number.

In the Hebrew language, each letter of the alphabet has a corresponding numerical value. While we do not know the specific name of the Antichrist, we do know that the numerical value of his name is 666. It may be that the Antichrist has already been born.

The Antichrist Is Satan's Co-conspirator

Revelation 13:1–4 describes a vision of the future regarding the Antichrist:

*I saw a beast rising up out of the sea, having seven heads and
ten horns, and on his horns ten crowns, and on his heads
a blasphemous name. Now the beast which I saw was like
a leopard, his feet were like the feet of a bear, and his mouth
like the mouth of a lion. The dragon gave him his power, his
throne, and great authority. And I saw one of his heads as
if it had been mortally wounded, and his deadly wound was
healed. And all the world marveled and followed the beast.
So they worshiped the dragon who gave authority to the
beast; and they worshiped the beast, saying, "Who is like
the beast? Who is able to make war with him?"*

The *"beast,"* another term for the Antichrist, is a formidable opponent—one who has governments under his control and powerful weapons at his disposal. Who is this *"dragon"* that grants authority to the beast, or the Antichrist? It is Satan, as attested in Revelation 12:9: *"So the great dragon was cast out, that serpent of old, called the Devil and Satan, who deceives the whole world; he was cast to the earth, and his angels were cast out with him."*

Satan seeks human worship through idolatry.

The word *"Devil"* means "slanderer"; the word *"Satan"* means "adversary." Ever desiring the worship of humans, Satan became God's adversary, aspiring to equality with Him and falling from heaven as a result. Satan wants to rival God by seeking human worship, which he obtains through idolatry. To achieve his ambition, he would even strike a deal with Jesus, which he attempted to do in Luke 4:5–8:

> *Then the devil, taking Him [Jesus] up on a high mountain, showed Him all the kingdoms of the world in a moment of time. And the devil said to Him, "All this authority I will give You, and their glory; for this has been delivered to me, and I give it to whomever I wish. Therefore, if You will worship before me, all will be Yours." And Jesus answered and said to him, "Get behind Me, Satan! For it is written, 'You shall worship the Lord your God, and Him only you shall serve.'"*

The true Christ rejected this deal proposed by Satan; the Antichrist will accept it. He will submit to Satan to gain dominion over the whole human race. When he gains this authority, he will receive worship, as will the one who empowered him—Satan.

The Role of Deception

To win worshipers to himself, Satan uses deception. Deception is something to which all are susceptible; no one should assume he or she is immune to it. As we have seen, those who withstand deception—and the sufferings inflicted by Satan—will receive eternal life. Adverse pressures will tempt us to stray from the faith, *"But he who endures to the end shall be saved"* (Matthew 24:13). my Jesus e love you

In a sense, the devil proves useful for God's purposes: God will use the devil's persecution of Christians to weed out uncommitted individuals so that the truly committed will stand. As Christ's bride, the church must be glorious, holy, spotless, and without blemish. Tremendous opposition will test and purify the church to prepare her for her wedding day, for union with her Bridegroom.

The Role of Pride

Satan also employs pride to win people's worship. Specifically, the movement known as humanism plays an instrumental role in cultivating confidence in human ability and talent. The motto of humanism is, "Man is the measure of all things." Denying an omnipotent deity, this movement deifies man and makes him the ultimate creature with unlimited capacity for knowledge.

Humanism rides the tide of the New Age movement, which denies all absolutes and embraces all philosophies and systems of thought under an umbrella of relativism. This movement rejects the cornerstone on which the Bible—and

119

all truth—is built: *"In the beginning God created the heavens and the earth"* (Genesis 1:1). God was the beginning, not man; He is the measure of all things, not man.

One final point about Satan's deception stems from Revelation 16:13: *"I saw three unclean spirits like frogs coming out of the mouth of the dragon, out of the mouth of the beast, and out of the mouth of the false prophet."* Here we find a satanic trinity that opposes the Holy Trinity: the dragon (versus God the Father), the beast (versus Jesus Christ the Son), and the false prophet (versus the Holy Spirit). As the ape of God, Satan can never create anything; he is utterly incapable of producing anything original. He can, however, corrupt and distort God's creation, hence his own counterfeit trinity of dragon, beast, and false prophet. This unholy trinity corrupts God's church to make a counterfeit version: the false church, or the harlot.

SPIRITUAL BLINDNESS BIRTHS DECEPTION

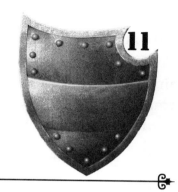

Nearly every passage in the New Testament that pertains to the end of the age includes some kind of warning about being deceived.

In Matthew 24:4–6, Jesus cautioned,

Take heed that no one deceives you. For many will come in My name, saying, "I am the Christ," and will deceive many. And you will hear of wars and rumors of wars. See that you are not troubled; for all these things must come to pass, but the end is not yet.

He added in verse 24, *"For false christs and false prophets will rise and show great signs and wonders to deceive, if possible, even the elect."*

The *"elect,"* or God's chosen ones, are not immune to deception. To avoid being deceived, we must be able to identify the truth. When Pontius Pilate interrogated Jesus before His crucifixion, Jesus told him, *"For this cause I was born, and for this cause I have come into the world, that I should bear witness to the truth. Everyone who is of the truth hears My voice"* (John 18:37). Pilate responded with a question philosophers have been asking—without a satisfactory answer—for twenty-five hundred years: *"What is truth?"* (verse 38).

The only satisfactory answer to this question is found in the Bible. The answer is not completely simple, however, because the Bible presents the truth in three facets. To ascertain that we have the truth, we must check each of these facets—I call them the "coordinates of truth." These three coordinates must align to confirm the truth.

The Coordinates of Truth

In John 14:6, Jesus said, *"I am the way, the truth, and the life."* Jesus is the truth. But in John 17:17, Jesus prayed to the Father, saying, *"Your word is truth."* God's Word—the Bible—is also truth. Finally, in 1 John 5:6, John wrote, *"It is the Spirit who bears witness* [to Jesus Christ], *because the Spirit is truth."* The Spirit is also truth. The truth is Jesus, the truth is the Bible, and the truth is the Spirit.

Jesus, God's Word, and the Spirit are truth.

To be sure that you are dealing with the truth, therefore, you must ask three questions. Is it true to Jesus? Is it true to the Bible? Does it have the witness of the Holy Spirit? If these questions are answered in the affirmative, you may be confident that you have the truth.

How Deception Displaces the Truth

Let us look again at Paul's warning about deception:

But I fear, lest somehow, as the serpent deceived Eve by his craftiness, so your minds may be corrupted from the simplicity that is in Christ. For if he who comes preaches

another Jesus whom we have not preached, or if you receive
a different spirit which you have not received, or a different
gospel which you have not accepted; you may well put up
with it!   (2 Corinthians 11:3–4)

How quickly we lose our grasp on the truth, letting go to
"put up with" false doctrine! I wrote earlier that Satan employs
deception and pride to win people's worship. Similarly, I
believe pride is the primary door through which deception
takes hold of our lives and misleads us.

Pride and Deception

Pride makes us susceptible to the snare of deception.
The pattern was set by Lucifer, who may have been the most
beautiful and wisest of the angels before pride made him
rebel, precipitating his fall from grace. If pride is able to so
destroy an archangel in heaven, how much more is it able to
destroy us who say, "It could never happen to me!" When
Satan wants to deceive us, he appeals to a surefire weakness:
our pride.

It is staggering how many cults make the same appeal
to pride. The Manifested Sons, a movement mentioned earlier, taught that people could achieve immortality by doing
the right things. The Mormons teach this, as do the Freema-
sons, however indirectly. These teachings may be traced back
to "The Lie," which Satan told to the human race when he
promised Eve that, by eating the fruit, *"You will be like God"*
(Genesis 3:5).

God purposely chooses those without pride to receive
His salvation and to understand His truth, as attested in 1
Corinthians 1:26–29:

For you see your calling, brethren, that not many wise according to the flesh, not many mighty, not many noble, are called. But God has chosen the foolish things of the world to put to shame the wise, and God has chosen the weak things of the world to put to shame the things which are mighty; and the base things of the world and the things which are despised God has chosen, and the things which are not, to bring to nothing the things that are, that no flesh should glory in His presence.

God plans to eliminate pride. He has chosen the foolish things, the weak things, the base or lowly things, and the things that are not (or nothing), so that no one can boast or say, "God chose me because I am so clever, so strong, and so wise. He needs me."

Do not make the same mistake I did as a young believer. As I mentioned earlier, when I was saved, I was serving in the British army in World War II. I was also a fellow of King's College, Cambridge; I had a distinguished academic record behind me and a bright future ahead of me. My attitude was puffed up and prideful; I actually thought that God was pretty lucky to get me. The more I learned about myself, however, the more I revised that opinion until I could say, "I cannot think why God would pick me!"

God has chosen the base and lowly things so no one can boast.

We must avoid anyone who promises that we will become "super-Christians" by joining a group or movement, for surely they appeal to our pride and reject the teachings of Jesus.

124

Deception and Self-Righteousness

Hand in hand with pride is another attitude that causes spiritual blindness: self-righteousness. In Romans, Paul wrote:

> *Brethren, my heart's desire and prayer to God for Israel is that they may be saved. For I bear them witness that they have a zeal for God, but not according to knowledge. For they being ignorant of God's righteousness, and seeking to establish their own righteousness, have not submitted to the righteousness of God.* (Romans 10:1–3)

The biblical definition of self-righteousness is attempting to establish one's own righteousness rather than relying on the righteousness God provides. Paul continued, *"Christ is the end of the law for righteousness to everyone who believes"* (verse 4). When this book and the Scripture passages herein mention the "law," they refer to the law code established by revelation from God to direct His people in their worship, their relationship to Him, and their social relationship to one another. Comprising many specific commandments and rules, this law was given in the Old Testament.

Christ's coming in the New Testament ended the law as a means of achieving righteousness with God. His death on the cross rendered the law eternally ineffective as a way to be righteous before God. No one—neither Jew nor Gentile, Catholic nor Protestant—can attain righteousness by fulfilling the law. I believe few Christians appreciate this fact, for many seem to live in the no man's land between law and grace. Unsure where they belong, they waive the benefits of both.

Israel should have known that personal righteousness will never suffice, for Isaiah explained this clearly: *"But we are all like an unclean thing, and all our righteousnesses are like filthy rags"* (Isaiah 64:6). Most people would probably expect Isaiah to have called our sins "filthy rags," but he actually used this metaphor to classify our righteousnesses—what we do in our attempt to achieve righteousness. As a result, Isaiah continued, *"We all fade as a leaf, and our iniquities, like the wind, have taken us away"* (verse 6). The barest amount of righteousness we might attain is no better than a filthy rag, and it is as inconsequential as a frail leaf carried by the wind.

For an example of self-righteousness in the Bible, turn to the parable Jesus told of a Pharisee praying in the temple:

> *Also He spoke this parable to some who trusted in themselves that they were righteous, and despised others: "Two men went up to the temple to pray, one a Pharisee and the other a tax collector. The Pharisee stood and prayed thus with himself, 'God, I thank You that I am not like other men; extortioners, unjust, adulterers, or even as this tax collector. I fast twice a week; I give tithes of all that I possess.' And the tax collector, standing afar off, would not so much as raise his eyes to heaven, but beat his breast, saying, 'God, be merciful to me a sinner!' I tell you, this man went down to his house justified rather than the other; for everyone who exalts himself will be humbled, and he who humbles himself will be exalted."*   (Luke 18:9–14)

These verses promise us that anyone who exalts himself will be abased, and anyone who humbles himself will be exalted. This creates a great paradox: the way up is down. The lower we go, the higher God will lift us. If we try to lift ourselves, however, God will surely frustrate our efforts and send us lower.

Five Distinct Features to Avoid

The self-righteous Pharisee in this parable exhibited five distinctive features worth considering.

1. Self-centeredness

The Pharisee was entirely self-centered, a key characteristic of self-righteousness. Having dealt with hundreds of people needing deliverance from demons, I have observed one characteristic common to each case: self-centeredness. This trait is a tactic of the devil, one to which the Pharisee succumbed. He trusted in his own righteousness, however illusory; and he *"prayed with himself"* (verse 11), wrapped up in his own words rather than the One to whom he would be wise to address them.

2. Disdain for Others

Second, the Pharisee felt superior to others, namely the tax collector praying nearby. Self-righteous people are so entirely wrapped up in themselves that they degrade and disdain everyone else.

3. Comparison with Others

Despising others stems from the practice of comparing ourselves with them. The Pharisee thanked God for making him different from the tax collector, but this sort of comparison is completely unscriptural. God does not compare us with others, and He does not condone this practice on our part, either.

4. Personalized Set of Rules

The fourth characteristic of the self-righteous Pharisee is that he used a tailor-made set of rules to justify his righteousness.

Instead of a list of positive practices, however, the Pharisee kept a list of negative behaviors he did not engage in. He was

A list of sins we do not commit does not make us righteous.

not unjust, he was not an extortioner, and he did not commit adultery. The two positive behaviors—biweekly fasting and faithful tithing—he believed reinforced his righteousness.

This trait is common, and it is especially pronounced when you confront someone about his or her sins. At the mention of sin, an automatic defense mechanism makes us protest and list the things we do not practice.

When I was saved while serving in the British army, the change in my life impressed many of my fellow soldiers. They would approach me for conversation, often broaching the subject of religion. I would talk to them about being saved, but the minute I brought up the issue of sin, they would protest, "I do not commit adultery!" or "I never beat my wife!" Each had his own list that suited his self-defense against the label of "sinner." This is exactly what the self-righteous Pharisee used.

5. Static Righteousness

Last, the Pharisee's "righteousness" was completely static, allowing no room for change or progress. He intended to continue as usual, living in compliance with his little list of rules but not expecting to improve (or acknowledging his need to do so).

Deception and Legalism

A friend of mine who is Catholic offered me a definition of legalism that I found particularly perceptive. He said that legalism makes the law an end in itself, losing sight of the real purpose for which the law was provided.

Trapped in his own rules and rituals, a legalist forgets why the law was given in the first place. Like someone who cannot see the forest for the trees, a legalist focuses on fulfilling specific rules and forgets their overarching purpose.

Why was the law given? The Bible provides a clear explanation in Matthew 22:35–40:

> Then one of them, a lawyer [a student of religious law; a theologian of sorts], asked Him a question, testing Him, and saying, "Teacher, which is the great commandment in the law?" Jesus said to him, "'You shall love the LORD your God with all your heart, with all your soul, and with all your mind.' This is the first and great commandment. And the second is like it: 'You shall love your neighbor as yourself.' On these two commandments hang all the Law and the Prophets."

By "the Law and the Prophets," Jesus was referring to what a contemporary Jew would call the Tanach, or the Old Testament. Jesus said that the entire Old Testament hangs on two commandments: to love God and to love your neighbor. To hang a garment on a peg, the peg must precede the garment; it has to be fastened to the wall before I can hang something on it. Thus, these two commandments—to love God and to love your neighbor—are primary; the law is secondary.

The purpose of the law relates directly to the two greatest commandments: it was given to produce a love for God and a love for neighbors. Any application or interpretation of the law that does not produce these two forms of love is a perversion of the law's intent. As Paul wrote in 1 Timothy 1:5, *"Now the purpose of the commandment is love from a pure heart, from a good conscience, and from sincere faith."*

Our common goal—the goal of our instruction and our striving—is love. If we swerve from that goal, we speak empty words and waste time, as Paul wrote in 1 Corinthians 13:1: *"Though I speak with the tongues of men and of angels, but have not love, I have become sounding brass or a clanging cymbal."*

The Example of the Sabbath

For an example of misusing the law via legalism in its truest sense, examine the attitude toward observation of the Sabbath in Jesus' day. Exodus 23:12 outlines the purpose of the Sabbath: *"Six days you shall do your work, and on the seventh day you shall rest, that your ox and your donkey may rest, and the son of your female servant and the stranger may be refreshed."* The words *"rest"* and *"refreshed"* express the primary purposes from a human standpoint for observing the Sabbath—a man and his household need a day for rest and refreshment. As Jesus stated in Mark 2:27, *"The Sabbath was made for man, and not man for the Sabbath."*

Legalism sometimes makes a burden of God's blessings.

The Pharisees inverted this statement so that man was for the benefit of the Sabbath instead of the Sabbath being for the benefit of man. This type of inverse is typical of legalism, which often takes what God has ordained for man's good and makes it a burden rather than a blessing.

In the gospels, it seems Jesus almost went out of His way to heal people on the Sabbath. After all, the purpose of the Sabbath was to bring rest and refreshment. How can someone who is crippled and contorted experience rest and refreshment? The religious leaders, however, wanted to keep those who suffered physically in their painful condition on the Sabbath just to be sure to observe the day properly. In doing so, they essentially twisted the Sabbath to accomplish the exact opposite of what God intended it to accomplish.

We see an example of this in Luke 13:11–16:

Behold, there was a woman who had a spirit of infirmity eighteen years, and was bent over and could in no way raise herself up. But when Jesus saw her, He called her to Him and said to her, "Woman, you are loosed from your infirmity." And He laid His hands on her, and immediately she was made straight, and glorified God. But the ruler of the synagogue answered with indignation, because Jesus had healed on the Sabbath; and he said to the crowd, "There are six days on which men ought to work; therefore come and be healed on them, and not on the Sabbath day." The Lord then answered him and said, "Hypocrite! Does not each one of you on the Sabbath loose his ox or donkey from the stall, and lead it away to water it? So ought not this woman, being a daughter of Abraham, whom Satan has bound; think of it; for eighteen years, be loosed from this bond on the Sabbath?"

Can you imagine a poor woman suffering with a physical ailment for eighteen years receiving a miraculous healing, only to incite the synagogue leader's indignation? The synagogue leader's self-righteousness was responsible for his outrage, and on a more serious level, his spiritual blindness.

In Matthew 23, Jesus arraigned the self-righteous religious leaders of His day, calling them, in succession, *"blind* guides" (verses 16, 24), "fools and blind" (verses 17, 19), and "blind Pharisee" (verse 26). The key word that characterizes them is blind, and I believe that self-righteousness inevitably produces spiritual blindness.

It is with the heart that we perceive spiritually.

In Romans 11:25, Paul explained Israel's mistake: "Blindness in part has happened to Israel until the fullness of the Gentiles has come in." The Greek word for "blindness" in this case means a hardness of heart, but a hardened heart relates closely to spiritual blindness, for it is with the heart that we perceive spiritually.

Spiritual blindness explains why many people—even regular churchgoers who are Christians and have been baptized in the Holy Spirit—are nearly blind to what God is doing. Self-righteousness not only produces spiritual blindness, but it also makes people blind to the reality of their condition.

Present-Day Legalists

Today we rarely deal with people who are trying to observe the Law of Moses. There are individuals who practice Orthodox Judaism, but this differs considerably from the Law of Moses in its strictest sense.

While most people may not rely on their fulfillment of the law, the Christian church contains a multitude of people who, like the Pharisee of the parable in Luke 18, have their own lists of rules they follow to reinforce, at least in their minds, their own righteousness. These people fit into five categories that I have identified.

1. Holiness Heritage

The first type of people who form their own personal lists come from what is known as a "holiness background." This background relates to Methodism, in particular, but it carries over into many sections of the Pentecostal movement, the Church of God, Pentecostal Holiness, and others. In their striving to achieve holiness, these people abide by a long list of strict, specific rules regarding issues as detailed as what women may wear, what people may eat and drink, where people may seek pleasure and entertainment, whether women and men may swim together…the list goes on.

While I was teaching a six-week Bible course at the leading Pentecostal assembly in Copenhagen, Denmark, I stayed at a home in the suburbs and would travel by streetcar to and from the city's center each day. By the streetcar stop in my neighborhood stood a statue of a man—Bishop Absalom—made of granite and metal. About three weeks into the course, I was growing weary of the Pentecostals' negative attitudes and finicky sets of rules, so I gave a lecture that centered on a familiar, local icon—the statue of Bishop Absalom.

Spiritual blindness blinds us to the reality of our condition.

"I want to tell you some things about Bishop Absalom," I said. "He does not smoke, he does not drink, he does not go to movies, he does not dance, he does not gamble, and he does not swear." I let the list sink in, then added, "But Bishop Absalom is not a Christian, because he has no life."

133

According to their standards, Bishop Absalom was impeccable. But he was also a lifeless statue, and life is the essence of Christianity. I think they got the message.

In Colossians 2:20–22, Paul wrote,

Therefore, if you died with Christ from the basic principles of the world, why, as though living in the world, do you subject yourselves to regulations; "Do not touch, do not taste, do not handle," which all concern things which perish with the using; according to the commandments and doctrines of men?

This passage provides a pretty accurate picture of holiness teaching. Do not misunderstand me—I am not saying that rules are necessarily wrong. Many of them are useful and good. What I am saying is that our righteousness does not consist in keeping those rules, especially when so many of them are sadly dated.

For example, when I was raising my family, radio was considered "worldly," so "good Christians" did not listen to the radio. We heeded this rule but had no inkling of television, and when television came along, no one had any rules against watching it.

Some people professed that Christians should not frequent movie theaters, but the advent of television brought movies into the home. Which is worse—engaging in "wrong" behavior outside your home or bringing something "wrong" into your home? Something "wrong" outside becomes twice as "wrong" inside, but our rules did not reflect this fact.

Another example pertains to women wearing makeup. For some time, a rule banned them from wearing lipstick.

This rule preceded the introduction of eye shadow, about which no rules were made. The wives of the Assemblies of God pastors, therefore, did not wear lipstick or rouge, but they wore so much eye makeup that they resembled ghosts. Our petty sets of man-made rules are often ridiculous and illogical.

2. Baptist Heritage

The second category reflects those with a Baptist heritage. The essence of their rules seems to be activity. You have to attend four meetings each week. You have to serve on three committees. You have to do door-to-door visitation. Inadequate participation condemns you. I personally think that Christians who spend excessive time at church—who go to church four or five times a week, for example—risk neglecting their families and homes.

Our righteousness does not consist in keeping rules.

I was formerly the associate pastor of an Assemblies of God church, where families would come at least five times a week for various functions, meetings, and services. This frequency seemed to foment frustration in families, and especially in younger children and teenagers, who became impatient for the day when they would never have to return to the church. They were weary of excessive activity.

In Romans 4:3, Paul wrote, *"For what does the Scripture say? 'Abraham believed God, and it was accounted to him for righteousness.'"* It was not what Abraham did, but what he believed—his faith in God—that qualified him as righteous.

If we are capable of achieving righteousness through works, then God owes us a reward. But God owes us nothing. *"But to him who does not work but believes on Him who justifies the ungodly, his faith is accounted for righteousness"* (verse 5). There are no outward acts that you can do to achieve righteousness, so abandon your futile efforts to do this or that. It is true that our good works reap eternal reward (see, for example, Matthew 16:27; Luke 6:35), but not if we do good works only in hopes of attaining righteousness. The only way to be righteous is to receive, by faith, the righteousness of God.

3. Fundamentalist Heritage

The third group forms its rules based on an obsession with the right doctrine. I call them the Fundamentalists. Fastidious about correct doctrine, they are eager to dot every "i" and cross every "t" if it means having the right answers. A lack of answers spawns insecurity, and to avoid this, Fundamentalists develop a defense of detailed doctrines to create a sense of security. If you challenge a Fundamentalist's doctrines, you undermine his security and provoke him to protest in self-defense.

Our security in God does not depend on our being right.

As I understand the gospel, our security in God does not depend on our being right. Even when we are wrong—which is much of the time—we can be secure if we are relying not upon ourselves, but upon God. There is much that we do not know; more still that we may never know. This is humbling, and it makes trying to be right in everything impossible.

136

4. "Spirituals"

People I refer to as "Spirituals" arise at five o'clock every morning, spend thirty minutes on their knees before an open Bible, and can spout countless Scripture passages by memory. They may even claim to receive revelations of things to come.

While these practices are positive, they cannot impart righteousness. Rising early to pray is good as long as you do not do it based on a feeling of obligation, or on the idea that it will make you righteous. I was once guilty of getting up early to pray because I thought I ought to, and what a futile effort it proved!

5. "Kitchen Counter Scrubbers"

The last group of rule-abiders comprises people whom I call "kitchen counter scrubbers." These people believe that righteousness consists of keeping the "kitchen" spotless— floor scrubbed, counters wiped, cupboards organized, dishes washed, corners dusted, napkins neatly folded, and so on.

When we focus on outward appearances, we neglect the reality within, where righteousness is administered and contained. People who trust themselves and keep a tidy exterior also tend to despise those whose kitchens are cluttered, people who do not abide by the same set of rules.

Kitchen counter scrubbers often grow prideful of their seemingly immaculate exterior, and this produces a dangerous spiritual condition. As Proverbs 16:18 warns, *"Pride goes before destruction, and a haughty spirit before a fall."*

The Antithesis of Self–Righteousness: God's Righteousness

Self-righteousness stems from man's natural desire to be self-sufficient. We value independence and strive to rely on ourselves rather than on God or on other people. One way people seek independence from God is by religion— establishing a strict protocol and following it as a means to righteousness. Man must accept his utter inability to achieve righteousness, thereby abandoning self-righteousness and surrendering to the righteousness of God—five aspects of which directly oppose the five aspects of self-righteousness we just looked at.

1. Christ–centered

While self-righteousness is self-centered, as the term suggests, God's righteousness is Christ-centered. To receive the righteousness of God, we have to divert our attention from ourselves and focus instead on Christ. Isaiah spoke on behalf of God in Isaiah 45:22: *"Look to Me, and be saved, all you ends of the earth!"* Incidentally, this applies not only to righteousness, but also to healing—many Christians suffer physically without relief because they focus on the symptoms instead of on the Lord. Christ is the Alpha and the Omega, the Beginning and the End, the First and the Last. (See Revelation 22:13.) We are complete in Christ, *"in whom are hidden all the treasures of wisdom and knowledge"* (Colossians 2:3).

2. Accepting of Others

Christ *"chose us in Him before the foundation of the world, that we should be holy and without blame before Him in love,…to the praise of the glory of His grace, by which He made us accepted in the*

Beloved" (Ephesians 1:4, 6). God's grace through Christ alone grants us righteousness; we can neither earn nor deserve it. We are accepted because of what Christ has done and because of who He is; we are beloved of God just as Christ is.

Because Christ has accepted us, we are to accept others instead of despising them, as self-righteousness causes us to do. We must treat others as God treats us.

If we live under the impression that God will accept us only as we keep His rules, we will accept others only as they keep the rules by which we abide. In contrast, if we live with the correct conviction that God freely accepts us in Christ and loves us unconditionally, we can freely accept other people and love them without establishing conditions they must fulfill.

Paul addressed this issue in Romans 14, where he talked about a man whose dietary choices were causing him to despise people who did not abstain from eating meat as he did: *"Let not him who eats despise him who does not eat, and let not him who does not eat judge him who eats; for God has received him"* (verse 3). God receives the people whom we despise.

> **Because Christ has accepted us, we are to accept others.**

Paul also instructed us, *"Therefore receive one another, just as Christ also received us, to the glory of God"* (Romans 15:7). We can learn how to receive others by understanding how Christ receives us. Does He tell us, "Get your life straightened out, follow this list of rules, and come back when you have accomplished this"? Absolutely not! Christ receives us as we are; it is not until He receives us that He begins to change us.

This order is significant. I am not suggesting that change is not necessary, but I am saying that receiving precedes changing. If we want to change someone, we must start by receiving him or her.

3. Looking to Jesus as the Sole Standard

Self-righteous people often compare themselves to others, but God has only one standard for righteousness: Jesus Christ. He uses no other standard to judge us. In 2 Corinthians 10:12, we read, *"We dare not class ourselves or compare ourselves with those who commend themselves. But they, measuring themselves by themselves, and comparing themselves among themselves, are not wise."* The opposite of wise is foolish; only fools measure themselves by others and form self-assessments based upon these comparisons.

Once I was scheduled to speak at a Wednesday night meeting at a church in Copenhagen, Denmark. I would have to speak through an interpreter who would translate my message from English into Danish for my audience. Speaking through an interpreter is tricky, however, because you have only a small margin for making sudden modifications or improvised jokes, which seldom translate easily across languages and cultures.

Jesus Christ is the sole standard by which God judges us.

I was under the impression that the purpose of this meeting was to share the gospel with a group of unbelievers. So I hunted for a text and decided upon 2 Corinthians 10:12. I planned to speak about the foolishness of comparing ourselves to other people because God has only one standard of judgment. I prepared my message and went to the church, only to discover that the meeting was actually for church members only. I was devastated. Lacking the experience and knowledge to alter my message, I preached as planned, speaking to the "saints" a message I had prepared for the "sinners."

The results were dramatic and unexpected: my message convicted these believers as never before. People were on their faces before the Lord, convicted because I had spoken exactly what they needed to hear and learn. My eyes were opened to realize that this message was not only for unbelievers, but also for believers who just as often compare themselves with other people.

Again, what is God's single standard by which He measures us? Acts 17:31 explains, *"He has appointed a day on which He will judge the world in righteousness by the Man whom He has ordained. He has given assurance of this to all by raising Him from the dead."*

God will judge neither our religious denominations nor our doctrines but our righteousness. The Man whom God raised from the dead is none other than Jesus Christ, who is both our standard and our judge. God has no standard besides Jesus, and if we measure ourselves according to another standard, we deceive ourselves.

4. Doing God's Will

God's righteousness does not consist of keeping a list of specific rules. Rather, when we believe God has accepted us, He is able to work in us, and our outward actions correspond accordingly.

I believe that God cannot work in us until we are absolutely sure of our acceptance, for it is by accepting us that God is able to work in us. Philippians 2:12–13 says,

> *Therefore, my beloved, as you have always obeyed, not as in my presence only, but now much more in my absence, work out your own salvation with fear and trembling; for it is God who works in you both to will and to do for His good pleasure.*

God works *in*; we work *out*. We depend completely on God's work within us, and His work is twofold: first to will, then to do, His good pleasure. We should naturally will to do that which is right, for God gives us the will to do it, then equips us with the ability to do so.

5. Lifelong Growth

Finally, God's righteousness is dynamic and progressive, not static or stationary. We grow in Christ as children in our Father's home.

The relationship between a human father and his child is a fitting illustration of this principle. A father would never say to his newborn baby, "When you learn all the rules, I will accept you as a child." On the contrary, fathers are delighted with newborn babies, and they accept them from birth. A child who grows up in a home where he is not accepted will encounter problems, while a child who is immediately accepted grows up desiring to do his father's will. Though he may fall and make mistakes, his father cannot reject him as his child. The father says, "You have made many mistakes, but come; we will start afresh."

Acceptance is the basis of our righteousness in Christ, and we receive acceptance not through works or rules, but from God in faith.

We move from acceptance into righteousness, growing in our resemblance to Christ. Ephesians 4:15 says, *"Speaking the truth in love, [we] may grow up in all things into Him who is the head; Christ."* A similar statement occurs in 2 Corinthians 3:18: *"But we all, with unveiled face, beholding as in a mirror the glory of the Lord, are being transformed into the same image from glory to glory, just as by the Spirit of the Lord."*

We change and undergo transformation, not thanks to our own effort, but thanks to the Holy Spirit, who imparts the glory of Christ. This process is ongoing; it lasts as long as our earthly life endures.

In Philippians 3:7–14, Paul spoke further of lifelong change:

But what things were gain to me, these I have counted loss for Christ. Yet indeed I also count all things loss for the excellence of the knowledge of Christ Jesus my Lord, for whom I have suffered the loss of all things, and count them as rubbish, that I may gain Christ and be found in Him, not having my own righteousness, which is from the law, but that which is through faith in Christ, the righteousness which is from God by faith; that I may know Him and the power of His resurrection, and the fellowship of His sufferings, being conformed to His death, if, by any means, I may attain to the resurrection from the dead. Not that I have already attained, or am already perfected; but I press on, that I may lay hold of that for which Christ Jesus has also laid hold of me. Brethren, I do not count myself to have apprehended; but one thing I do, forgetting those things which are behind and reaching forward to those things which are ahead, I press toward the goal for the prize of the upward call of God in Christ Jesus.

Our Ultimate Goal

Our ultimate goal is Christ's righteousness, which He alone imparts through the Holy Spirit. As Proverbs 4:18 teaches, *"But the path of the just ["righteous" NIV] is like the shining sun, that shines ever brighter unto the perfect day."*

If we are walking the pathway of the righteous, the light should grow brighter every day as we grow closer to God. If the light by which I live today is no brighter than it was yesterday, I am in danger of backsliding, of relying on self-made methods and rules instead of God's righteousness. This type of backsliding promotes self-righteousness, which must be avoided if we want to prevent spiritual blindness and subsequent deception.

DEFEAT SATAN'S
DECEPTIVE SCHEMES

You must make an honest self-evaluation to gauge the degree to which you are susceptible to deception, for only then can you arm yourself against Satan's tactics. These characteristics are not exhaustive, but are rather the most prominent features of people who are most likely to be deceived.

Characteristics of Candidates for Deception

Reliance on Subjective Impressions

Subjective impressions—formed from emotions, intuition, and senses—generate conclusions that are often ill-founded and incorrect. Subjective evaluations are highly suspect, skewed by our sinful nature and biased minds.

Someone might say, "When so-and-so prophesied for me, I felt so good. His message must have been from God." This type of evaluation is dangerous because it stems solely from sentiment. Many tests are more important than how you feel about something.

Looking Only to Human Leaders

Some people place complete trust in human leaders, whether they are pastors, priests, prophets, or spiritual mentors. No human leader is infallible. Believing everything anyone says without checking it against Scripture or testing it in other ways is dangerous.

Accepting Supernatural Signs as a Guarantee of Truth

Jesus Himself said that false prophets will arise and perform great signs and wonders—the key word is false. The mere fact that a sign is supernatural does not suffice as a guarantee of its authenticity.

False prophets exist, and Satan is capable of supernatural signs and wonders, too. As we have discussed, anyone who accepts these things blindly and assumes they come from God is sure to succumb to deception.

Unwillingness to Face Suffering or Persecution

The Bible warns us that as believers, we must expect to face persecution and suffering for our faith. Peter wrote, *"Since Christ suffered for us in the flesh, arm yourselves also with the same mind, for he who has suffered in the flesh has ceased from sin, that he no longer should live the rest of his time in the flesh for the lusts of men, but for the will of God"* (1 Peter 4:1–2).

Second Timothy 3:12 likewise tells us, *"All who desire to live godly in Christ Jesus will suffer persecution."* Suffering is a reality of the Christian life. God uses it to shape us. Anyone who expects or promises only good things is a false prophet or a misled individual.

Ignorance of Scripture

Some people in remote, unreached countries do not have a Bible; they have only a word—perhaps the teachings of missionaries or a spoken explanation of the gospel. God will be merciful to them. But for those of us who have Bibles at our ready disposal, neglecting to study them sets us up for deception. By arming ourselves with the truth as expressed in God's Word, we can avoid much deception. But if we remain ignorant about His truths and teachings, we deserve to be deceived.

A Series of Safeguards

Now that you have a better understanding of what makes people susceptible to deception, you will be more equipped to recognize falsehoods and resist deception. To foil the schemes of Satan, practice the following four safeguards when you are tempted by pride, when you encounter signs and wonders, or when your awe of God wanes.

These safeguards, paired with a close, personal relationship with Christ, will guard you from deception and enable you to maintain your membership in the true church.

1. Humility

The first safeguard may be found in 1 Peter 5:5–6: *"God resists the proud, but gives grace to the humble.' Therefore humble yourselves under the mighty hand of God, that He may exalt you in due time."* Humility consists in exalting God and putting others first rather than seeking to exalt ourselves. This quality is essential if we expect to come into the presence of God.

Neglecting to study our Bibles sets us up for deception.

The Bible never says that God will make us humble; it is our responsibility. People can preach to us and pray for us, but the ultimate decision to practice humility must be

147

our own. Psalm 25:8–9 provides encouragement: *"Good and upright is the LORD; therefore He teaches sinners in the way. The humble He guides in justice, and the humble He teaches His way."* It is thanks to His grace that the Lord teaches sinners at all. God does not enroll students based on intellectual qualifications, but on character. Many people may attend Bible school or seminary, but they cannot register for classes in God's school unless they humble themselves.

2. Receive the Love of the Truth

The second safeguard stems from a warning in 2 Thessalonians 2:9: *"The coming of the lawless one* [the Antichrist] *is according to the working of Satan, with all power, signs, and lying wonders."*

Never underestimate Satan's ability to produce power, signs, and wonders. Most charismatics attribute anything supernatural to God, which is why I have identified the charismatic movement as a likely place for the Antichrist to emerge.

How can we protect ourselves from being deceived by Satan's supernatural signs and wonders? We must receive a love of the truth. In 2 Thessalonians 2:10, we see that *"unrighteous deception"* will ensnare *"those who perish, because they did not receive the love of the truth, that they might be saved."* God offers us a love of the truth, and we must accept it to be saved. Cultivating a love of the truth entails more than reading your Bible daily, going to church, and hearing sermons. It means having a passionate commitment to the truth of God.

> *God offers us a love of the truth, and we must accept it.*

To those who reject a love of the truth, 2 Thessalonians 2:11–12 says, *"For this reason God will send them strong delusion, that they should believe the lie, that they all may be condemned who did not believe the truth but had pleasure in unrighteousness."*

When God sends delusion, it deludes without fail. Should He delude someone, there are two possible ways to pray: first, that God will work through the delusion to accomplish His purposes; second, that God will protect us from succumbing to the delusion ourselves.

God chastens those He loves.

People are deluded when they are governed by the soulish nature. Two key words that appeal to the soulish nature are *peace* and *love*. Everybody clamors for peace, something contingent—according to the Bible—on righteousness. Apart from righteousness, peace cannot exist. In Isaiah 48:22, the prophet wrote, *"'There is no peace,' says the Lord, 'for the wicked.'"* Politicians use the word peace to win supporters, but this amounts to manipulation, because peace will not come to the unrighteous.

The word *love* is used frequently in the church to manipulate individuals. They emphasize that "God is love," which is true. Yet while God is loving, He is also strict; He forgives, but He also holds us accountable for our actions, thoughts, and words. A sentimental concept of God as Father Christmas, doling out candy to little children, is far from His actual righteousness and holy severity. Again, God chastens those He loves; He fulfills His promise to discipline His children.

When God rebukes us in love, we must respond appropriately so that we will continue to cultivate our love for the truth. Hebrews 12:5–8 explains the incorrect response to God's discipline:

> You have forgotten the exhortation which speaks to you as to sons: "My son, do not despise the chastening of the LORD, nor be discouraged when you are rebuked by Him; for whom the LORD loves He chastens, and scourges every son whom He receives." If you endure chastening, God deals with you as with sons; for what son is there whom a father does not chasten? But if you are without chastening, of which all have become partakers, then you are illegitimate and not sons.

We must neither despise nor be discouraged by the Lord's chastening. As we accept and respond positively to God's discipline, we will safeguard ourselves from deception.

3. Cultivate the Fear of the Lord

I want ✓

The fear of the Lord is crucial in the Christian life. Fear of God, or "fear of the Lord," to the Christian, is a feeling of reverence, awe, and respect of God. The unbeliever has every reason to be panic-stricken in his fear of God because he stands condemned before Him. Psalm 34:11–14 reads,

> Come, you children, listen to me; I will teach you the fear of the LORD. Who is the man who desires life, and loves many days, that he may see good? Keep your tongue from evil, and your lips from speaking deceit. Depart from evil and do good; seek peace and pursue it.

Additional Scriptures about the fear of the Lord include Psalm 19:9—*"The fear of the LORD is clean, enduring forever"*—and Job 28:28—*"Behold, the fear of the Lord, that is wisdom, and to depart from evil is understanding."*

150

The requirements of the fear of the Lord are not intellectual, but moral. Clever fools abound; we must depart from evil and instead do what is right. Proverbs 8:13 teaches, *"The fear of the LORD is to hate evil; pride and arrogance and the evil way and the perverse mouth I hate."* The fear of the Lord requires a hatred of evil; you must despise pride and arrogance. In this way, you will not leave the door open for spiritual blindness and deception.

The fear of the Lord requires us to despise pride and arrogance.

When we fear the Lord, He promises us a long life of blessings and wisdom, as stated in Proverbs 9:10–11: *"The fear of the LORD is the beginning of wisdom, and the knowledge of the Holy One is understanding. For by me your days will be multiplied, and years of life will be added to you."*

The fear of the Lord also provides comfort and confidence: *"In the fear of the LORD there is strong confidence, and His children will have a place of refuge. The fear of the LORD is a fountain of life, to turn one away from the snares of death"* (Proverbs 14:26–27).

Fearing the Lord does not guarantee an easy, carefree life, but it does promise satisfaction: *"The fear of the LORD leads to life, and he who has it will abide in satisfaction; he will not be visited with evil"* (Proverbs 19:23).

One final passage of importance is the prophetic picture of the Messiah presented in the eleventh chapter of Isaiah:

There shall come forth a Rod from the stem of Jesse, and a Branch shall grow out of his roots. The Spirit of the LORD shall rest upon Him, the Spirit of wisdom and understanding,

the Spirit of counsel and might, the Spirit of knowledge and
of the fear of the LORD. (Isaiah 11:1–2)

The New Testament Scriptures confirm that this *"Branch"* is Jesus Christ, and it is significant to note that the Spirit resting on Him is sevenfold. The number seven is always associated with the Holy Spirit. One example is in Revelation 4:5, which speaks of seven lamps of fire—the seven Spirits of God—that are before the throne of God.

> *Knowledge*
> *puffs up*
> *pride; fear*
> *of the Lord*
> *makes us*
> *humble.*

I believe the above passage from Isaiah reveals the nature of the seven Spirits of God. The first, the Spirit of the Lord, is God Himself. His nature is then described in pairs: the Spirit of wisdom and understanding, the Spirit of counsel and might, and the Spirit of knowledge and of the fear of the Lord. This last pair underscores the importance of balancing knowledge—which tends to puff up our pride—with a fear of the Lord, which tends to make us humble.

The fear of the Lord serves to counterbalance "happiness," a sentiment often disconnected from faith. In the charismatic movement, especially, people clap their hands and dance with excitement—this is positive only when paired with a respectful fear of the Lord. Fear accompanied the growth of the church, described in Acts 9:31: *"Then the churches throughout all Judea, Galilee, and Samaria had peace and were edified. And walking in the fear of the Lord and in the comfort of the Holy Spirit, they were multiplied."* God comforts us and builds us up, but we must fear Him with deep reverence.

Some people mistakenly assume that being saved makes the fear of the Lord obsolete and unnecessary. On the contrary, believers should respect and reverence God even more because of the tremendous price He paid to redeem them. As 1 Peter 1:17–19 states,

> *If you call on the Father, who without partiality judges according to each one's work, conduct yourselves throughout the time of your stay here in fear; knowing that you were not redeemed with corruptible things, like silver or gold, from your aimless conduct received by tradition from your fathers, but with the precious blood of Christ, as of a lamb without blemish and without spot.*

When we value the fear of the Lord, we guard against pride, ingratitude, and taking God for granted.

4. Surrender to the Centrality of the Cross

In 1 Corinthians 2:1–3, Paul wrote,

> *I, brethren, when I came to you, did not come with excellence of speech or of wisdom declaring to you the testimony of God. For I determined not to know anything among you except Jesus Christ and Him crucified. I was with you in weakness, in fear, and in much trembling.*

In Paul's day, oratory prowess was the utmost achievement; unskilled public speakers were derided and despised. To show that he relied only on Christ and His atoning work on the cross, Paul highlighted his own inability and weakness.

As he emphasized in 2 Corinthians 12:9, God's strength is made perfect in man's weakness. God must bring us to the place where our strength fails so that we learn to rely on the strength He provides. Otherwise, we again will lean on our own perceived sufficiency and may fall into the snares of self-righteousness.

When our strength fails, we learn to rely on the strength God provides.

My own ministry testifies to this truth: to use me in any significant way, God had to bring me to the point of incapability, where I acknowledged my dependence upon His strength, perfected in my weakness. When I prepared to preach, I would pray to God, "I know I do not have the ability. I am totally dependent upon You. If You do not anoint me, if You do not inspire me, if You do not strengthen me, I cannot do it."

In 1 Corinthians 2:4–5, Paul continued,

My speech and my preaching were not with persuasive words of human wisdom, but in demonstration of the Spirit and of power, that your faith should not be in the wisdom of men but in the power of God.

Focusing on the cross is essential to release the power of the Holy Spirit.

In 1707, Isaac Watts wrote the popular hymn "When I Survey the Wondrous Cross," the first verse of which states, "When I survey the wondrous cross,/ On which the Prince of Glory died,/ My richest gain I count but loss,/ And pour contempt on all my pride." When we truly focus on the cross, we realize we have nothing to boast of.

The Baptist preacher Charles Spurgeon continually emphasized focusing on the cross. He once made an analogy

154

to illustrate the importance of this focus. In essence, he said that preaching the principles of the Christian life without mentioning the cross is like a drill sergeant giving orders to a squad of soldiers without feet. They can comprehend his orders but are incapable of carrying them out. It is through the cross alone that we have the ability to accomplish God's purposes for us.

When Paul excused himself for his weak oratory skills, he also excused his limited wisdom—by this, he meant a lack of familiarity with Greek philosophy. In Acts 17, Paul was in Athens, a university city that formed the intellectual center of ancient times. Adapting to his audience, Paul preached an intellectual sermon, possibly even quoting a Greek poet. His results, however, were nominal; few people believed his message.

Next, Paul went to Corinth (see Acts 18), a major port city rife with sin and wickedness. It was apparently between Athens and Corinth that Paul reached his decision to abandon human skill and wisdom to rely on the strength of God. Forgetting everything else, Paul made Christ crucified—the cross—the center of his message. Surrendering personal claims to power or ability, Paul allowed the Holy Spirit

The cross alone makes us able to accomplish the purposes God has for us.

to come in power and to speak through his weakness. This happened when he made the cross his central focus.

If we practice the safeguards we have discussed, it will make us less susceptible to deception. In the next chapter, we will continue with some suggestions of ways to keep ourselves from being deceived.

Cultivate

A Life in Christ

I t goes without saying that a personal relationship with Christ is necessary if we are to thwart the schemes of the devil.

First and foremost, we must cultivate a love of the truth, for in doing so we love God and seek His Word, which is truth.

In 2 Thessalonians 2:9–10, we learn that loving the truth will protect us from the Antichrist:

> The coming of the lawless one is according to the working of Satan, with all power, signs, and lying wonders, and with all unrighteous deception among those who perish, because they did not receive the love of the truth, that they might be saved.

If we reject the love of the truth, we are bound to perish. The word *"love"* in this case means more than just tolerating the truth or allowing someone to present the truth to us. It means seeking the truth, finding it for ourselves.

We must take time to read our Bibles and to bask in the presence of the Lord. Time spent in His presence equips us to recognize the truth and to reject everything else.

Give God Your Time

Spending time in fellowship with other Christians is important, but more important still is spending time alone with God. Many people devote a negligible amount of time to God. They should repent and change their ways.

My wife Ruth and I regularly took one day each week—we chose Wednesday—to wait on God. We had no preconceived notions of what would happen; we had neither agenda nor prayer list. Sometimes we would begin by reading the Bible; other times we would not. But by the end of the day, we always asked, "How did we ever get here?" God always surprised us with where we were and what we were doing at the end of the day.

At one point, Ruth and I took a six-month sabbatical from November to April. We went to Hawaii, deeming it an appropriate place to be renewed and refreshed. We had just finished a certain phase of our life and ministry, having passed the reins of Derek Prince Ministries to David Selby, his competent staff, and the board of directors. Waiving all responsibilities except prayer, we headed to Hawaii with the purpose of seeking God's direction and trusting Him to prepare and equip us for the next phase. We made no commitments; I did no preaching.

Many people devote a negligible amount of time to God.

What we anticipated as a relaxing time turned into one of the most difficult and trying periods I have ever endured. My health declined significantly; I spent two and a half weeks in a hospital with a heart condition that was, until recently, incurable. Had it escaped

158

diagnosis, I might have died in Hawaii. I thank God for providing doctors, nurses, and medical treatment, as well as people to support and pray for us.

During this time, God provided a clear sense of the direction our ministry was to take: from then on, we were first and foremost to engage in intercession, prayer, worship, and waiting on God. This final instruction—waiting on God—was an appropriate lesson learned by doing just that. Had we set aside only four or five months

We should not expect to hear from God if we refuse to give Him our time.

for our sabbatical, we might not have received an answer. For five and a half months, God was silent about the answer. He taught us many things, but it was not until the last two weeks that He revealed the answer to what we were seeking to know.

God's other lessons to us during the sabbatical dealt with time as well. God wants our time, and if we refuse to devote time to Him, I do not think we should expect to hear from Him. God wants not just any time, but open-ended time. Instead of saying, "Lord, we will give You the next half-hour or the next half-day," we should say, "Lord, we will give You time until we hear from You, no matter how long it takes."

Many people are impatient to hear from God. You might ask, "Why did you have to wait five and a half months to hear from God?" First, God is sovereign: He does what He wants, when He wants, the way He wants. He does not require our permission or sanction. He answers in His timing. Second, God revealed to us many personal, internal barriers we needed to dismantle before He could speak and show us His way. He took five and a half months to deal with those barriers, leading us through a process of confession, repentance, and self-humbling. Self-humbling is often crucial; it is an action rather than a feeling.

Someone once said, "Humility is not something you are; humility is something you do." Rather than trying to feel humble, we must practice humility by putting others first and thinking of our needs as less important. The results will follow.

Be Humble

I have already emphasized the importance of humility, which comes when we remove the barrier of pride—a barrier that can inhibit communication with God. One way to humble ourselves before God is by confessing our sins.

1. Confess to God *Father God forgive me*

In 1 John 1:9, we read, *"If we confess our sins, He is faithful and just to forgive us our sins and to cleanse us from all unrighteousness."* God does not want to hold your sins against you, which is why He provided a way for you to receive complete cleansing and forgiveness.

There is one condition, however: we must confess our sins. If we do not confess them, they still count against us. Our sole escape is through confession, acknowledging the ways we have wronged God.

I want to discourage you, however, from launching a process of painstaking self-examination, for the more you examine yourself, the less you will like yourself. God has provided an examiner: the Holy Spirit. Jesus said that when the Holy

Halleluah !!!

Spirit comes, He will convict us of sin, of righteousness, and of judgment. As John wrote in 1 John 5:17, *"All unrighteousness is sin."* Anything that is not righteousness is, by default, sinful. The distinction is black and white, with no gray area; the Holy Spirit convicts us of anything that is not righteousness. The Holy Spirit does not, however, cause us to feel guilty; only Satan instills guilt and makes us doubt whether we have done enough to compensate for our sin.

2. Confess to Others

The second key to humility is found in James 5:16: *"Confess your trespasses to one another, and pray for one another, that you may be healed."* In the Christian life, unconfessed sins pile up and prevent us from receiving healing. We can humble ourselves by confessing our sins to God, and sometimes more so by confessing them to other people. This self-humbling is healthy and is based on scriptural instruction. My wife Ruth and I confessed many things to one another; I believe neither one of us withheld any known sin from the other.

Apologizing humbles the wrongdoer and heals the victim's heart.

Some years ago I was counseling a man who was unreasonably angry with his wife and children. He was a Christian who earnestly desired to serve and obey the Lord. I recommended that every time he lost his temper, he confess that specific sin to them; the more he did that, the less likely he would be to lose his temper again. I believe many marriages would benefit from the shared confession of sins between husband and wife. Acknowledging wrongdoing and apologizing for it humbles the wrongdoer and heals the heart of the victim.

3. Submit to God's Dealings

A third way to humble ourselves is to submit to God's dealings. In Deuteronomy 32:3–4, Moses proclaimed, *"Ascribe greatness to our God. He is the Rock, His work is perfect; for all His ways are justice, a God of truth and without injustice; righteous and upright is He."* God is just; it is impossible for Him to be either unjust or unfair. Let us not deceive ourselves by thinking that He owes us something. God makes no mistakes, and we cannot call Him unfair just because He fails to fulfill our hopes and desires.

We will all experience "unfair" situations in life. We may lack sufficient financial resources; our friends may betray us. How are we to respond? In 1 Peter 5:6, we are told, *"Humble yourselves under the mighty hand of God, that He may exalt you in due time."* Instead of presuming to know what is best for us and growing bitter when something else happens, we must humble ourselves.

We must pray to God, "Father, I do not understand what is happening, but I know You are perfectly just. You never make mistakes. What You do is right, and I submit to Your dealings. Teach me what I do not know, and help me to understand Your ways."

When God brought Israel out of Egypt, He allowed them to pass through great trials designed to humble them. In Deuteronomy 8:2–3, Moses said,

You shall remember that the LORD your God led you all the way these forty years in the wilderness, to humble you

and test you, to know what was in your heart, whether you would keep His commandments or not. So He humbled you, allowed you to hunger, and fed you with manna which you did not know nor did your fathers know.

How did God humble the Israelites? He let them pass through times of apparent need and insufficiency, when their carnal desires were not satisfied. His purpose was to humble them, but the process was prolonged—instead of humbling themselves, one generation perished in the wilderness because they complained, muttered, rebelled, and ultimately blamed God.

If we humble ourselves, the purposes of God will be fulfilled.

When we encounter a difficult time, we must not mutter or whine; nor should we accuse God of unfairness, or we will miss His purpose. If we humble ourselves, God's purposes will be fulfilled.

When my first wife, Lydia, and I had to emigrate from Israel to Britain, we were homeless; our eight girls were divided among different homes, and we were miserable. God spoke, though, and said, "Humble yourselves under the mighty hand of God." It took some time to follow this order, but the result was beneficial. When things go wrong and our wishes are not fulfilled, we should humble ourselves. We must acknowledge God's fairness and ask Him to show us the way of obedience.

Job 7:17–18 is an amazing passage of Scripture addressed to the Lord: *"What is man, that You should exalt him, that You should set Your heart on him, that You should visit him every morning, and test him every moment?"* We undergo continual testing to determine whether we are faithful and obedient or rebellious and disobedient. God tests us every moment and visits us every morning; we must remain open to His guidance.

Four Necessary Changes

The words of John the Baptist preparing the way for Jesus in Isaiah 40:3–5 prove an appropriate closing to this topic:

> *The voice of one crying in the wilderness: "Prepare the way of the LORD; make straight in the desert a highway for our God. Every valley shall be exalted and every mountain and hill brought low; the crooked places shall be made straight and the rough places smooth; the glory of the LORD shall be revealed, and all flesh shall see it together; for the mouth of the LORD has spoken."*

Just as John the Baptist spoke these words in preparation for Jesus' first coming, I believe God speaks these words to us to prepare us for Jesus' return. This passage ends with the promise that the glory of the Lord will be revealed, and all flesh will see it. How do we prepare the way of the Lord? We must remove the barriers that we erect to resist God's purpose and plans.

God tests us every moment and visits us every morning.

Four changes must occur, illustrated by the landscape imagery: (1) Every valley shall be exalted; (2) every mountain and hill shall be brought down; (3) the crooked places shall be made straight; (4) the rough places shall be made smooth. What is low must be raised up; what is high must be reduced. Our hype and exaggeration, our self-aggrandizement and boasting, must cease; we must practice humility. Self-exaltation and self-promotion will hardly hasten God's arrival. He will reward virtues that contemporary society seems to despise: modesty, chastity, self-effacement, servitude.

We must choose to be channels of God's glory.

Any crookedness in our lives must be straightened; rough places must be smoothed. Our egoism, our tendency to react resentfully when things run against what we prefer, our argumentativeness—these should be ironed out.

Preparing to Be Useful to God

As we undergo trials—personally as individuals, collectively as a church—God prepares us to receive the revelation of His glory, which will occur because His Word says so, and He is faithful to fulfill His Word. His glory will be revealed only through those who have met His conditions—conditions established in the Scripture passage above.

I believe God is working to bring about the fulfillment of this Scripture. More specifically, He is working to bring it about in the church of this nation. We must choose to be either channels for His glory or mountains that withstand it. A time of testing is upon us; in fact, it has started in the lives of many whom God has tested with trials and tribulations.

God never uses anything or anyone without initial testing, so if we want to be of use in His kingdom, we must expect to undergo and pass a test. Let us resolve to persevere through tests, keeping in mind the blessings that will follow if we make the grade. We should not lose determination or

165

drop out, but should rather expect tests and rely on God's grace to pass them.

CHRISTIAN LIVING
IN THE PRESENT EVIL AGE

I n the last two chapters, we learned how to avoid being susceptible to deception by practicing a series of safeguards against Satan's schemes and preparing ourselves to be used by God in the times in which we live. The ultimate protection from deception will occur when Jesus returns again, His kingdom reigns over all the earth, and Satan is cast out forever. As we will learn, the Bible describes the period of human history that leads up to this time as *"this present evil age"* (Galatians 1:4). This is the age in which we are currently living. In our final chapters, we will learn more about the nature of the present age, how it will culminate with Christ's return, and how to remain faithful to God until the dawn of this day.

Are We Different?

Until the end of this age arrives, we are to await Christ's coming and to resist deception. How many of us are truly prepared for the end? I fear that a great number of people in America who claim to be born-again Christians are making a regrettably poor impression. When John the Baptist introduced

Jesus and the gospel, he said, *"Even now the ax is laid to the root of the trees"* (Matthew 3:10; Luke 3:9).

When God deals with a situation, He does not bother with the branches or the trunk. No, He goes straight for the root. When you deal with the root, you no longer have problems with the tree that grows from it.

Someone gave me a secular publication produced by a reputable marketing research firm. The publication had no spiritual overtones or religious themes; its sole concerns were dollars and cents. The research this publication dealt with was none other than "How to Market to Born-Again Christians." It addressed questions such as these: "What must one say and do to market to Christians? How can you persuade them to make purchases? After all, so-called born-again Christians compose a significant sector of the buying market."

As I read this survey, which spanned about four pages, I could tell that the analyst had spent significant time in close quarters with born-again Christians. He knew exactly what he was talking about.

The ultimate message of the survey is that there is no significant difference between born-again Christian consumers and others who are not in this category. Distinctions were negligible, according to the research, conclusions, and counsel of this highly qualified, secular observer.

A Disturbing Conclusion

This reality should be disturbing to us. As Christians, we are to be in the world, but not of the world. (See John 17:14–16.) Should not our passions, practices, and purpose mark us as radically different from people who do not profess our faith, people who love the world and think that nothing exists beyond it?

A simple illustration provides a pithy parallel to our situation: a ship in the sea is all right; the sea in a ship is all wrong. In the same way, the church in the world is all right; the world in the church is all wrong. If there is too much of the sea in a ship, it will sink. I believe the ship of today's church is so near sinking that every individual who becomes a believer and accepts Christianity is set to bailing water with everyone else to keep the church afloat.

Christians are to be in the world but not of the world.

Many of us come to church with needs. If we focus merely on our needs, we will never come to the end of them; rather, we will live with them forever. Something must release us from a myopic focus on our own needs, drawing us beyond the realm of "I need, I want, help me, pray for me, bless me." As long as we dwell on such things, we remain enslaved by them. We need to press past a self-centered focus to acquire the wisdom of God.

I once heard someone define wisdom as "seeing things from God's perspective." In many cases, Christianity is quite similar to astronomers' beliefs about the solar system in the days before Galileo. Early thinkers such as Aristotle and Ptolemy propounded a geocentric model of the universe: the earth was at the center of the solar system, and the sun revolved around it. This perception prevailed until the Italian astronomer Galileo overturned it with the heliocentric model. This view incurred immediate reproof—from the Catholic Church, no less—and Galileo was forced to recant and was put under house arrest by the Inquisition.

Many Christians today are spiritually as the Aristotelian model of the universe—we often think that God revolves around us, that Jesus Christ, His Son, rises and sets around us. We are earth-centered and self-centered. I believe that we require a spiritual revolution to move us from Aristotle to Galileo, to the point where we realize that the Son does not revolve around us. Rather, we revolve around the Son.

The ultimate purpose of everything is not related to us; it is related to God, who is both beginning and end. The world may not recognize this truth, but we, as Christians, do, and should reflect the centrality of God in the way we live.

I believe the church needs a total revolution. God remembers the faithfulness of the ancestors of the American people. I think this generation has spent just about all of its spiritual inheritance, and it is time for God to receive a return on His investment.

This World Is Ending

Let us look once more at a passage in the book of Galatians, where Paul wrote,

> *Grace to you and peace from God the Father and our Lord Jesus Christ, who gave Himself for our sins, that He might deliver us from this present evil age, according to the will of our God and Father.* (Galatians 1:3–4)

Do we understand why it is imperative for us to be delivered from this present evil age? Our deliverance is already taking place, but we must make our calling sure. (See 2 Peter

1:10.) We do not belong to this age; we belong to the next age. Let us consider the solemn truths written in Hebrews 6:4–6:

> *For it is impossible for those who were once enlightened, and have tasted the heavenly gift, and have become partakers of the Holy Spirit, and have tasted the good word of God and the powers of the age to come, if they fall away, to renew them again to repentance, since they crucify again for themselves the Son of God, and put Him to an open shame.*

This passage raises many theological issues, but I personally believe what it says. It is possible to come to a point where one has forfeited any further hope in Christ. I think this applies not only to backsliders, but also to people who turn and actually deny Jesus Christ, even after having known Him, and treat Him irreverently.

This passage speaks of people who have had several experiences. They have been enlightened. The Holy Spirit has shown them the truth. They have tasted the heavenly gift (which is the gift of eternal life in Jesus Christ). They have become partakers of the Holy Spirit. Through faith in Jesus they have received the Holy Spirit. They have tasted the Word of God and have known its truth, reality, and power to nourish and sustain.

What we call supernatural in this age will be natural in the next age.

The passage then mentions *"the powers of the age to come."* When we are baptized in the Holy Spirit, we begin to taste a small part of what will be normal in the next age. What we call supernatural in this age will be natural in the next age. God gives us a foretaste so that we have an idea of what it will be like.

An Abundant Entrance

Because of this foretaste, we should not expect the experience of passing out of time and moving into eternity to feel entirely foreign or strange. In his second epistle, Peter wrote about having an abundant entrance into the kingdom of God:

> *Therefore, brethren, be even more diligent to make your call and election sure, for if you do these things you will never stumble; for so an entrance will be supplied to you abundantly into the everlasting kingdom of our Lord and Savior Jesus Christ.* (2 Peter 1:10–11)

What a desirable way to enter into eternity! I heard a story of a woman who was in a prayer meeting where the minister was teaching those assembled to pray prophetic prayers for one another. Someone prayed that this woman would see the church as Jesus sees it; afterward, whenever anyone mentioned the word *church*, she burst into tears. I think the man's prayer was answered.

Jesus will return for one bride, one church.

I was driving through a town one day and was particularly struck by the number of different churches I passed. I thought, Is this what God intends? I do not believe so. Jesus is no bigamist; He is not returning for more than one bride. He will not return for a Catholic church or a Protestant church or a charismatic church.

The dividing line between the true church and the false church at the end of this age will not be determined by whether we speak in tongues. Rather, it will be a matter

172

of faithfulness to the Bridegroom. Have we been faithful or unfaithful? As was discussed in earlier chapters, we will either be the bride—a member of the true church—or the harlot—a member of the false church. No alternatives exist.

Avoiding Conformity to the World

The Bible teaches clearly that we must not conform to the present age. In Romans 12:2, Paul wrote, *"Do not be conformed to this world, but be transformed by the renewing of your mind, that you may prove what is that good and acceptable and perfect will of God."*

As long as we think the same way this age thinks, we cannot discern the will of God for our lives. Countless Christians are stumbling around, wondering what God has in store for them. They fail to find it because they think the way the world thinks. They share the world's values, motives, priorities, and standards. God does not reveal His will to such minds.

Self-centeredness

The natural mind is self-centered. It always asks, "What will I get out of this? What will this do for me? What will people say about me?" The renewed mind, on the other hand, is God-centered. It always asks, "Will this please God? Will this glorify Him? Will this expand the kingdom of God?"

As long as we remain self-centered, we are prisoners of ourselves. Adopting a God-centered mind liberates us from slavery to selfishness and allows us to seek the glory of His kingdom.

I have counseled many people who required frequent deliverance. Do you know what I discovered? People who have numerous and persistent problems with demons are typically self-centered. They will spout off their problems without realizing that, by doing so, they are constructing the bars of their own cages. Their primary problem is self-centeredness.

Self-sacrifice in marriage must be mutual.

This issue has also caused the breakup of many marriages between so-called Christians. When two spouses are self-centered, their marriage cannot stand, for both ask, "What will I get out of this? What will my spouse do for me?" By asking these questions, they fail to meet the conditions for a successful Christian marriage. Christian marriages begin with a life laid down for one's mate. This self-sacrifice must be mutual. Many marriages of Christians—even of Christian pastors—are breaking down because of the presence of the world within the church.

Worries

In the parable of the sower in the book of Matthew, we read, *"He who received seed among the thorns is he who hears the word, and the cares of this world and the deceitfulness of riches choke the word, and he becomes unfruitful"* (Matthew 13:22). We learn here that one characteristic of this age is that it impresses cares and worries on us.

These worries, while sometimes trifling, are nonetheless significant because they can keep us from being ready to meet the Lord. In Luke 21:34, Jesus said, *"But take heed to yourselves, lest your hearts be weighed down with carousing, drunkenness, and cares of this life."* Such cares command our attention and distract our focus, preventing us from being prepared for the next age.

Let me tell you, dear brothers and sisters, that if we are full of worries, it is because we are living in the wrong age. This age is replete with worries; the next age is devoid of them. One cannot help worrying when he lives in the wrong age. Interestingly enough, even the fruits of technology—things like computers, which were invented to make life easier—tend to complicate life and add to our worries.

When I was a missionary in Africa, Iris Sheehan, one of my fellow missionaries, directed a school for girls. Iris was a hard-working missionary, and she believed in having all the best equipment, including a washing machine and clothes dryer. Her students would say to her, "Miss Sheehan, you must have such an easy life when you have a washing machine and a dryer." These girls could not imagine how someone with such modern conveniences could have any worries. How many of you know better?

If we are full of worries, we are living in the wrong age.

Material goods do not reduce our worries, regardless of their being designed to do so. I am not opposed to them, but I will maintain that if we want to be free from worry, we must live in a different age. We must know experientially what it means to have been delivered from *"this present evil age"* (Galatians 1:4).

Petty, Frivolous Rules

In my experience with the Pentecostal tradition, I became intimately familiar with its set of rules: clothing you must not wear, places you must not go. Many people who observe these rules still react to situations as the world does. While they have changed a few minor external details, such as fashion and pastimes, their thinking has not changed in the slightest.

When God changes someone, He does not start with the exterior, giving commands to remove makeup or to wear long dresses. Instead, He starts with the interior, changing the way people think. Once He changes our thinking, He does not have to worry about our conduct; it will align naturally with our thinking.

Colossians 2:13–15 says,

You, being dead in your trespasses and the uncircumcision of your flesh, He has made alive together with Him, having forgiven you all trespasses, having wiped out the handwriting of requirements that was against us, which was contrary to us. And He has taken it out of the way, having nailed it to the cross. Having disarmed principalities and powers, He made a public spectacle of them, triumphing over them in it.

What was the written code, or the *"handwriting of requirements,"* with its regulations? The law. If you study the book of Galatians, you find that because the Christians in Galatia had lost sight of the cross, they went back to abiding by the law (or at least trying to). Paul asked them, in effect, "How can you be so stupid? Having begun in the Spirit, are you now being made perfect by the flesh?" (See Galatians 3:3.)

This is what happens to Christians who lose sight of the cross. It describes the history of the church, as well as the history of nearly every denomination in the church. They began in the Spirit, lost sight of the cross, ceased to believe in the supernatural, and returned to a system of rules and regulations.

We who are so "spiritual" say that we are not under the Law of Moses, yet we persist in making our own silly little laws. The Baptists have a set of laws, the Pentecostals have another, the Catholics have yet another. No set of laws can make us righteous before God. Christianity is not a set of rules, but rather a personal relationship with the Lord.

We say that we are not under the Law of Moses, yet we persist in making silly laws.

I fear that the majority of Christians in America do not realize that Christianity is not a set of rules. How has this happened? The cross and what it achieved have been obscured. Once we lose sight of the cross, we have lost everything, really. We may not lose our salvation, but experientially we lose the ability to enjoy what God has provided for us.

The crux of the gospel message is that people cannot achieve righteousness by keeping a set of rules. God has written off the rules. As Paul wrote in Romans 10:4, "*Christ is the end of the law for righteousness to everyone who believes.*" It makes no difference whether you are Protestant or Catholic, Jew or Gentile. We must understand that Christ is not the end of the law as the law relates to the Word of God or Israel's culture and history or as a revelation of the wisdom of God. Yet Christ is the end of the law as it relates to righteousness. If we try to achieve righteousness by following a set of rules, we are telling Jesus, "You died in vain. You did not need to die." What a terrible thing to do!

Through the death of Jesus, God made provision for our sins—sins past, present, and future. All of our past sins are forgiven, but even that is not enough. We can have our sins forgiven and still fall short of eternal life.

I was raised in the Anglican Church, and I appreciate tremendously the prayer book that we used at weekly services. Every Sunday morning, we would proclaim the General Confession, which said, "Pardon us, miserable offenders. We have erred and strayed from Thy ways like black sheep. We have done that which we ought not to have done, and have left undone that which we should have done."

I had no difficulty acknowledging that truth with the rest of the congregation. But later, especially when I was a teenager, my problem was that when I left the building after church, I kept doing the same things I had been asking God to forgive. It is essentially insulting God to confess sin, ask Him to forgive, and then say, "As a matter of fact, God, I am going to continue committing the same sins You have forgiven." For years, I refused to feel like a true "miserable offender" until God convicted me.

> *People could not come completely to God until the law was set aside.*

People could not come completely to God and live in His favor until the law had been set aside. Every time anyone would attempt to do the right thing, Satan would negate the validity of the attempt, citing all the rules the person had broken in the meantime. The number of things one would have to do to keep the law is staggering. None of us can do it successfully. The secret of the cross is that Jesus removed the law as a requirement for achieving righteousness with God. Thank You, Lord! Hallelujah

I now walk in the ways of God, although I often stumble; I have many weaknesses and problems. I need not worry as long as I continue to believe, though, for my faith is reckoned to me as righteousness. (See Romans 4.) As long as I remain in the faith, God says, in effect, "I will take responsibility for you."

We are considered righteous because of our faith.

I am particularly impressed by the exchange between Jesus and Peter at the Last Supper, when Jesus told Peter that he would deny Him three times. Jesus said to Peter, *"I have prayed for you"* (Luke 22:32). He did not say, "I have prayed for you that you will not deny Me." Rather, Jesus told Peter, in effect, "I have prayed for you that your faith will not fail. Even if you deny Me, if you do not surrender your faith, I will retrieve you." (See verse 32.) Is this not wonderful news? Our faith is counted to us as righteousness. As long as we believe in the One who gave Jesus to die for our offenses and who raised Him from the dead for our justification, we are considered righteous.

I feel an inner sigh of relief every time I think about this truth. I thank God that I do not have to keep all sorts of silly rules. There is a place for rules; do not misunderstand me. Every church is entitled to make its own rules by which its members must abide. If you are a church member, you have an obligation to observe the rules of your particular church. But we do not achieve righteousness with God by observing any set of rules.

The problem with Christians is that each group has its own set of rules, and they consider themselves righteous when they keep those rules, condemning others who do not keep them.

Love of the World

A final problem in our dealing with the present age is discussed in 2 Timothy. Paul instructed Timothy, *"Be diligent to come to me quickly; for Demas has forsaken me, having loved this present world, and has departed for Thessalonica"* (2 Timothy 4:9–10).

What was Demas's problem? He loved the present age. From two additional epistles, we know that Demas had been a trusted coworker of the apostle Paul and had been with him through many situations. Paul was clearly unaware of this character flaw, so he must have been quite shocked to learn of Demas's love for this world.

Love of the present age is a fatal flaw.

Demas probably had a long list of reasons to break company with Paul: Paul was getting old and growing feeble; he was in jail; the days when he had stirred entire cities with his sermons had passed. One of his closest associates, Trophimus, was ailing, and Paul had left him behind in Miletus, unable to even pray him back to health. By worldly standards, Paul was a failure. Demas measured according to the world's standards, concluding, "This is a sinking ship; I had better get off while I can."

I would not suppose that, having parted company with Paul, Demas entered a life of sin. He was not pursuing prostitutes or frequenting bars. He just wanted a more secure and reasonable kind of life. His mistake was not one we typically preach against. Had he been an abject sinner, Paul would not have kept him as a fellow worker. Demas's one fatal flaw was his love for the present age, but this had been latent for years.

Could it be that we harbor the same love, that we have the same flaw? It is remarkable what people can get by with in the world today, but what the world accepts, God rejects. There will come a time in every life when everyone will be tested, and they will pass, assuming they do not have this fatal weakness of a love for the present age.

We must not condemn Demas unless we are absolutely sure that we would not have done the same thing he did. Suppose we had been with Paul. He is in prison; he is manacled; it is getting cold and wintry…would we have deserted him, too? I believe that if we do not practice laying down our lives daily, we will not lay them down when the big moment arrives. Those who lead self-pleasing, self-centered lives now will not be able to make the right decision when the final moment comes.

CHRISTIANS ARE AT ODDS WITH THE WORLD

The world does not recognize Jesus or His disciples. As John 1:10 attests, *"He [Jesus] was in the world, and the world was made through Him, and the world did not know Him."* Why did the world not know Jesus? Because their eyes had been blinded by Satan.

In 1 John 3:1, we read, *"Behold what manner of love the Father has bestowed on us, that we should be called children of God! Therefore the world does not know us, because it did not know Him."* If the world does not know our elder brother, Jesus, the world does not know the other members of His family.

We should not worry if the world does not know us. It did not know Him, either. In fact, we should worry if the world thinks too well of us. If it does, we may be in danger.

Hated by the World

The next statement goes further, saying that the world actually hates Jesus and His followers. In John 15:18–19, Jesus told His disciples,

If the world hates you, you know that it hated Me before it hated you. If you were of the world, the world would love

its own. Yet because you are not of the world, but I chose you out of the world, therefore the world hates you.

Notice that in verse 19, the phrase *"the world"* occurs five times. Jesus must have meant what He was saying.

In John 17:14, Jesus prayed for His disciples, saying, *"I have given them Your word; and the world has hated them because they are not of the world, just as I am not of the world."*

Brothers and sisters, we must not worry if the world hates us. Rather, we should take heart, because if the world loved us as its own, we would belong in the wrong company. I do not mean to suggest that we go around looking for persecution, but I do mean that we must be realistic. Sooner or later, the world will hate us.

Opposite Spirits

The Spirit of God and the world are completely at odds with one another. First Corinthians 2:11 says, *"What man knows the things of a man except the spirit of the man which is in him? Even so no one knows the things of God except the Spirit of God."* The sole source of revelation of the things of God is the Holy Spirit.

Paul continued in verse 12, *"Now we have received, not the spirit of the world, but the Spirit who is from God, that we might know the things that have been freely given to us by God."* It is not the spirit of the world, but rather the Spirit of God, who makes known to us the things of God. The spirit of the world and the Spirit of God are opposites.

I once had a problem when dealing with nice, charismatic people. Most of them loved me. They believed the Bible, and they were not leading openly sinful lives. But when I began to minister to them in certain areas, I found a strong, invisible force coming against me. The pressure of this force was tremendous and almost physically painful. Although these people were believers, they were slow to grasp spiritual truth. I thought, *Whatever am I dealing with?*

The spirit of the world can still control religious people.

God showed me the answer in 1 Corinthians 2:11—I was dealing with the spirit of the world. Even in these good people, the spirit of the world reigned. They had little time for God and for prayer; they spent more time watching television than reading the Bible. Unwilling to make any significant sacrifice, they always put their own convenience before the things of God.

My eyes were opened to realize that you can be as religious as you please, but the spirit of the world can still control you. My wife and I decided to pray for these people, and as we did, things started to improve.

In 1 Corinthians 2:13, we read, *"These things we also speak, not in words which man's wisdom teaches but which the Holy Spirit teaches, comparing spiritual things with spiritual."* This verse is significant. No human discipline—such as philosophy, psychology, or psychiatry—acknowledges the reality of the Spirit. But man is spirit, soul, and body. Any attempt to classify man that excludes the reality of the spirit distorts the truth.

When I hear preachers quote famous psychologists, I sometimes fear what they will say. God's Word does not need to be endorsed by psychologists or psychiatrists. It does its own job. God's Word is alive, powerful, and sharper than any two-edged sword. It divides soul from spirit; in fact, it is the only thing that can do so.

Hebrews 4:12 says,

For the word of God is living and powerful, and sharper than any two-edged sword, piercing even to the division of soul and spirit, and of joints and marrow, and is a discerner of the thoughts and intents of the heart.

God's Spirit Is Greater

The good news is that the Spirit of God in believers is greater than the spirit of the world. Hallelujah! First John 4:1–6 says,

Beloved, do not believe every spirit, but test the spirits, whether they are of God; because many false prophets have gone out into the world. By this you know the Spirit of God: Every spirit that confesses that Jesus Christ has come in the flesh is of God, and every spirit that does not confess that Jesus Christ has come in the flesh is not of God. And this is the spirit of the Antichrist, which you have heard was coming, and is now already in the world. You are of God, little children, and have overcome them, because He who is in you is greater than he who is in the world. They are of the world. Therefore they speak as of the world, and the world hears them. We are of God. He who knows God hears us; he who is not of God does not hear us. By this we know the spirit of truth and the spirit of error.

"He who is in you" is the Holy Spirit. The spirit in the world is the spirit of Antichrist. Thank God that we are on the winning side! While I do not believe we are going to take over the world, I do believe we will not be defeated by Satan.

186

Worldly people hear the spirit of this world. We must present the truth in the power of the Holy Spirit, but we cannot meet the world on its own terms.

Let me illustrate by asking an important question concerning the church and Hollywood. Which has exerted greater influence over the other? Has the church influenced Hollywood, or has Hollywood influenced the church?

In Hollywood, we find the spirit of the world. This spirit embraces the spirit of competition—big names and headlines. If you look in any newspaper at the page where churches advertise their Sunday services, you will see that many of these churches make claims in the spirit of competition, such as "We have the biggest choir" or "We have the best preacher." This competitive clamoring exhibits the spirit of the world.

We are trying to meet the world on its own terms, and this should not be done. We must not bow to the world.

When we stop being impressed by what the world thinks, and when we stop adhering to the world's standards and values, we cease to be slaves to the world. What a liberating experience! Instead of working to please the world, we can live to please

> *Many churches make claims in the spirit of competition.*

God. Now, I do not advise going out of your way to offend people; I believe we should be gracious, tactful, and humble, but we should not bow to the god of this world.

Focus on the Eternal

As we read in 1 Corinthians 2:12–14, the Spirit of God reveals the things of God. But the spirit of the world ridicules the things of God, which are foolishness to anyone who lacks the Spirit. In John 16:13–14, Jesus said that when the Spirit of truth has come, *"He will glorify Me."* This is a foolproof test of whether the Holy Spirit is at work. Is the movement or method under consideration glorifying to Jesus? If not, we can be sure that it is not of the Spirit of God.

The Holy Spirit focuses our minds on eternity.

The spirit of the world focuses on man, preparing the world for the Antichrist. The philosophy of humanism fuels this focus on man; it holds that man is the measure of all things, and that nothing higher than man exists, making man equal to a god.

Hebrews 9:14 says, *"Christ…through the eternal Spirit offered Himself without spot to God."* The Holy Spirit is the *"eternal Spirit"*; the Greek word for this term means spirit of all the ages, a spirit that is not limited or bounded by time.

Paul wrote,

Our light affliction, which is but for a moment, is working for us a far more exceeding and eternal weight of glory, while we do not look at the things which are seen, but at the things which are not seen. For the things which are seen are temporary, but the things which are not seen are eternal.

(2 Corinthians 4:17–18)

The eternal Spirit reveals eternal things. He focuses our minds on eternity—the real, permanent issues of life and death. The spirit of this world, on the other hand, focuses our minds on the things of time, which endure only temporarily.

188

The spirit of this world does not want to acknowledge that anything exists beyond us. It is afraid of that idea.

Jesus said in John 16:8, *"When He* [the Spirit of truth] *has come, He will convict the world of sin, and of righteousness, and of judgment."* These eternal realities—sin, righteousness, and judgment—are the realities on which true religion is based. At the end of our lives, we will give an account to God, and as the Bible says, *"All unrighteousness is sin"* (1 John 5:17).

What we have done is either sinful or righteous; there are no alternative categories. As Paul wrote in 2 Corinthians 5:10, *"We must all appear before the judgment seat of Christ, that each one may receive the things done in the body, according to what he has done, whether good or bad."* There is no in-between.

If there is one word the world hates, it is the word accountable. The essence of humanism is the rejection of accountability and personal responsibility. Humanists deny accountability to anyone, holding that everything is relative. No one has to answer to anyone for anything. Peter described this perspective when he wrote about what will happen at the end of the age:

> *Scoffers will come in the last days, walking according to their own lusts, and saying, "Where is the promise of His coming? For since the fathers fell asleep, all things continue as they were from the beginning of creation."* (2 Peter 3:3–4)

Scoffers will mock the promise of the Lord's return; this is the "wisdom" of the world.

Second Timothy 1:7 says, *"God has not given us a spirit of fear, but of power and of love and of a sound mind."* The *"power"* this passage refers to is not political, physical, or military;

rather, it is spiritual power—power over evil. The spirit of this world is the spirit of subjection to evil, but the Spirit of God brings love to overpower evil. The spirit of this world brings strife, disharmony, and hatred. Yet Hebrews 10:29 calls the Holy Spirit the *"Spirit of grace."*

Overcoming the world also means not being corrupted by worldly lusts.

The only way that grace enters our lives is through God's Holy Spirit. The spirit of this world is the opposite of grace; it is the spirit of fleshly effort, the spirit of people who struggle, practice self-reliance, and believe they can pull themselves up by their own bootstraps.

To summarize, the spirit of this world, the *"spirit of error"* (1 John 4:6), completely opposes the Spirit of God, the Spirit of truth. The Spirit of God reveals the things of God—truths that are mocked and reviled by the spirit of this world. The spirit of this world focuses on man, but the Spirit of God focuses on Jesus. The Spirit of God convicts of sin, righteousness, and judgment, while the spirit of this world denies the real and lasting significance of these things. One day, we all will give an account to God. Praise Him who makes us righteous.

Avoid the Corruption of Lust

As we saw earlier, overcoming the world also means not being corrupted by the world's lusts. Second Peter 1:3–4 says:

[God's] *divine power has given to us all things that pertain to life and godliness, through the knowledge of Him who called us by glory and virtue, by which have been given to*

190

us exceedingly great and precious promises, that through these you may be partakers of the divine nature, having escaped the corruption that is in the world through lust.

In this passage, we learn that we will not have to ask God for anything; He has given it already. All we must do is discover the promises and claim them, because they are there for the taking. *"Through these* [the promises of God's Word] *you may be partakers of the divine nature* [the nature of God Himself], *having escaped the corruption that is in the world through lust."*

Our divine destiny is to become partakers of the nature of God, and to do so more and more. The more of God's Word we take in, the more we acquire the nature of God, thus partaking of His nature. The more we partake of God's nature, the less likely we are to become corrupt, because the divine nature cannot accommodate corruption; they are completely incompatible.

> *The more we partake of God's nature, the less likely we are to be corrupted.*

In the New Testament, lust is a word with a specific meaning: perverted, inordinate desires. Man was created with only good desires, but when he turned against his Creator and rebelled, those good desires were perverted. The gratification of these perverse desires leads to corruption.

If we look at the world today, we see that it is manifestly corrupt through perverted desires. People are doing the most senseless things that destroy their bodies. Take smoking, for example. This is a lust. I do not condemn people who smoke, but I am sorry for them, for they are only destroying themselves. This perverse desire brings corruption—a practical corruption, at that—lung cancer, tongue cancer, emphysema, to name a few of its effects.

We cannot love both the world and the Father.

In 1 John 2:15, we are instructed, *"Do not love the world or the things in the world. If anyone loves the world, the love of the Father is not in him."* We cannot love both the world and the Father. This is an issue of either-or, for love of the world and love of God are mutually exclusive. Verse 16 continues, *"For all that is in the world; the lust of the flesh, the lust of the eyes, and the pride of life; is not of the Father but is of the world."* Again, the love of Father and love of the world are incompatible.

Three Aspects of Lust

In verse 17, we read, *"The world is passing away, and the lust of it; but he who does the will of God abides forever."* The world is corrupt through lust, three types of which John delineated in verse 16: the lust of the flesh, the lust of the eyes, and the pride of life.

An analysis of temptation as it is recorded throughout the Bible shows that it takes these three forms—lust of the flesh, lust of the eyes, or the pride of life. Temptation began with Eve, when Satan enticed her to taste the forbidden fruit. Genesis 3:6 says, *"When the woman **saw** that the tree was good for food, that it was **pleasant to the eyes**, and a tree desirable to make one wise, she took of its fruit and ate"* (emphasis added).

The beginning of Eve's problem was her moving out of the realm of faith and into the realm of the senses. Instead of

192

believing what God had said, she went by what she saw. This precipitated her downfall. The only way back is the inverse: renouncing the guidance of fallible senses and believing instead the Word of God.

Eve's temptation corresponds to the lusts specified in 1 John 2:16: *"good for food"* (lust of the flesh), *"pleasant to the eyes"* (lust of the eyes), and *"desirable to make one wise"* (the pride of life; the desire to exalt oneself). If we analyze the nature of this temptation, we will find that it was not a temptation to do evil, per se. The temptation was to be like God.

Independence from God

The essence of this temptation was the desire for independence from God. As long as we desire in our hearts to be independent of God, we occupy a dangerous position. Nothing in this created universe has any right to be independent of its Creator, God.

Adam and Eve believed they could achieve independence by gaining knowledge. The desire to know was not wrong, in itself, but the desire to know as a means of gaining independence was the root of their problem. I know many Christians who have not dealt with the desire to be independent of God.

Nothing in this created universe has a right to be independent of its Creator.

The pride of life causes individuals to say, "I can manage my life without God. If I am in a real emergency, I may pray, but in general, I can handle the situation." Some people treat the Holy Spirit like an emergency vehicle or 9-1-1 number. When all else fails, they pray. This is not the way we were designed to live. We were designed to live in an hour-by-hour, moment-by-moment dependence on the Spirit of God.

Three Temptations

Satan tempted Jesus with three temptations that correspond to these three lusts. Let us read the account in Matthew 4:1–10.

> *Then Jesus was led up by the Spirit into the wilderness to be tempted by the devil. And when He had fasted forty days and forty nights, afterward He was hungry. Now when the tempter came to Him, he said, "If You are the Son of God, command that these stones become bread." But He answered and said, "It is written, 'Man shall not live by bread alone, but by every word that proceeds from the mouth of God.'" Then the devil took Him up into the holy city, set Him on the pinnacle of the temple, and said to Him, "If You are the Son of God, throw Yourself down. For it is written: 'He shall give His angels charge over you,' and, 'In their hands they shall bear you up, lest you dash your foot against a stone.'" Jesus said to him, "It is written again, 'You shall not tempt the Lord your God.'" Again, the devil took Him up on an exceedingly high mountain, and showed Him all the kingdoms of the world and their glory. And he said to Him, "All these things I will give You if You will fall down and worship me." Then Jesus said to him, "Away with you, Satan! For it is written, 'You shall worship the Lord your God, and Him only you shall serve.'"*

Satan first tempted Jesus to turn stones into bread. Appealing to the lust of the flesh, Satan invited Jesus to do like so many who put their stomachs before obedience to God. It is strange that in our churches, alcoholism is frowned on, while gluttony is tolerated or even encouraged. There is no real difference, for both are deadly. I am inclined to think that overeating can likely kill someone as quickly as alcohol, perhaps even more quickly. It is incredible how our traditions blind us to facts.

Satan's second temptation showed Jesus the kingdoms of the world and their glory in a moment of time, appealing this time to the lust of the eyes. Think of the sparkle and the splendor; think of the crown, the pearls, the diamonds, the luxury. Satan said that all Jesus had to do was fall down and worship him, and He would receive all these riches.

Jesus is the true Messiah, the true Christ; as such, He rejected this deal. As we discussed in an earlier chapter, the false christ will accept the deal. He will fall down and worship Satan in exchange for promises of power and luxury and riches; he will bow to Satan. Christ would not.

I do not think error enters the church except by pride.

The third temptation invited Jesus to cast Himself down from the pinnacle of the temple, to perform a miracle displaying the immeasurable amount of His power—the pride of life. This may be the subtlest of all temptations—the temptation to use one's spiritual gifts for self-promotion. This happens often in the church, and the underlying essence of the sin is pride.

I do not think error enters the church except by pride. All religious error stems from pride. If someone wants to generate a following, one can do just that by making promises of greatness to people, by making them feel exclusive and superior.

The Process of Corruption

An additional point of interest is that Adam fell through eating, while Jesus overcame by fasting. When we deal with our stomachs, we have dealt with the root. Fasting, when rightly practiced, is effective for spiritual growth.

When I was saved, I knew I had to fast; I did so every Wednesday for four and a half years. I do not believe I could have ever become what God intended me to be without learning, early on, the secret of fasting.

Jesus overcame temptation by fasting. We must therefore avoid the corruption of lust that controls the world. When something becomes corrupt, it is impossible to eradicate the corruption, be it fruit, flesh, or anything else. Consider, for example, a Georgia peach. If you put it on a shelf and leave it there for one week, it will begin to wither and turn yellow, losing its pleasant aroma and flavor. Once this happens, you cannot reverse the process or restore the fruit's freshness. You can put the peach in the refrigerator to slow the corruption process, but you still cannot reverse it.

I think some churches act like refrigerators, slowing but not stopping the corruption of the fruit they contain—their congregations. The corruption may not be rapid or glaring, but it is still there. This is true of the world, too; there is nothing to reverse the process of corruption.

God is not going to change the world; He is going to replace the world. This is what He does in our lives. Sin corrupts us, so we must be born again. He gives us a new start. He does not patch up or repair our old, corrupted selves; rather, He makes us new beings with a new, divine origin and an incorruptible life. We must live holy lives in keeping with this life.

Avoid Contamination by the World

Believers must use, but not abuse, the world. There can be a fine line between these two words—use and abuse. In 1 Corinthians 7:31, we read, *"Those who use this world as not misusing it. For the form of this world is passing away."* The *New International Version* says, *"Those who use the things of the world, as if not engrossed in them."* In other words, we must not let the world grab hold of us. We should keep the world at arm's length, interacting with it but never allowing it to master or possess us.

As we proclaim the gospel, we must not be contaminated by the world, which contains vast amounts of pollutants—spiritual contaminants. The book of James exhorts us concerning spiritual purity. The Bible has little to say about religion, but it has a lot to say about salvation. The difference is that religion is what people do for God, while salvation is what God does for people.

We should keep the world at arm's length.

When it comes to religion, if more people would read James 1:26–27, our churches might be much different. Verse 26 says, *"If anyone among you thinks he is religious, and does not bridle his tongue but deceives his own heart, this one's religion is useless."* It does not matter whether we call ourselves Baptists, Catholics, or Pentecostals—if we do not control our tongues, our religion is without value. Some people may have never realized this before.

In the next chapter, we move from avoiding the corruption of the world to the amazing influence God's people will have upon the world.

CHRISTIANS ARE
THE LIGHT OF THE WORLD

I n Matthew 5:14, Jesus told His disciples, *"You are the light of the world."* As I wrote earlier, I believe that the Holy Spirit working through the church is the sole source of light in this darkened world. Do not confuse education or enlightenment with light, because you can be completely educated and still remain in the dark. I can say this with authority because it once applied to me. I had the best education Britain could offer; I was an academic success, but spiritually, I was completely in the dark.

Another important Scripture passage about the church's influence in the world is Philippians 2:15–16, where Paul wrote about his hope,

> *that you may become blameless and harmless, children of God without fault in the midst of a crooked and perverse generation, among whom you shine as lights in the world, holding fast the word of life.*

The last phrase—*"holding fast the word of life"*—is crucial. We shine only insofar as we hold forth the *"word of life."* Whatever calling God gives to each of us, we must shine in these areas, holding forth the word of life in some measure.

As we proclaim the good news, we shed light in the world and share hope with a dark and perishing generation.

Believers Represent Jesus in Word and in Deed

As believers, we are to be Jesus' representatives in the world. I heard the testimony of a man who served in the British navy during World War II. He was an adamant unbeliever who was assigned to a small naval ship with only a few fellow personnel, one of whom was a Christian. The unbelieving man disliked the Christian and wanted to keep a distance between them, but there was no place to escape him on that small ship. The unbeliever would not read his Bible, but he had no choice but to "read" the life of the Christian man, with whom daily interaction and intimacy was inevitable. By his life and character, the Christian man convinced the unbeliever of God's existence.

You may be the only Bible someone will ever read.

Remember: you may be the only Bible someone is ever going to read. There may be someone at your workplace, someone in your neighborhood, or someone at the grocery store who never opens a Bible but who looks at your life and can see a reflection of God.

First John 4:17 says, *"As He is, so are we in this world."* The world does not see Jesus, but the world does see us who believe in Him. They should see us as being as Jesus is.

Not only are we to model Jesus, but we are also to proclaim the gospel message to the entire world. In Matthew 24:3, the disciples asked Jesus, *"What will be the sign of Your coming, and of the end of the age?"* Notice that they asked to know *"the sign"*—not signs, plural, but *"the sign,"*singular.

In His response in the verses that follow, Jesus gave them a list of signs—among which were *"famines, pestilences, and earthquakes in various places"* (verse 7)—but He had yet to answer the question. In verse 14, He finally concluded, *"This gospel of the kingdom will be preached in all the world as a witness to all the nations, and then the end will come."* This is a specific answer to a specific question.

What will signify the end of the age? The gospel will be proclaimed in all the world as a witness to all the nations. When this has come to pass, the end will follow. Along with the various signs Jesus promised, the tell-tale sign of the end of the age consists of the gospel's being spread throughout the world.

Christians Must Spread the Gospel Message

Who is responsible for proclaiming the gospel? We are. We must understand that the destiny of many people hinges on us and on what we do. Their eternal destiny is not in the hand of the military leaders, politicians, or scientists. These people cannot bring the end of the age. We alone, as Christians, are responsible.

At the end of the age, the gospel will spread throughout the world.

Recall that Satan is the god of this age. He does not want the age to end, for when it does, he will cease to be a god. Therefore, Satan does everything in his power to delay or postpone the end of the age. We are responsible for seeing that the age is brought to God's appointed climax. We do not do this by merely sitting in church and singing hymns but by proclaiming the gospel. I do not think the devil really objects to most churches. You might think I am being cynical, but I think Satan sees churches as an effective way of keeping most Christians harmlessly and fruitlessly occupied.

I once heard a rather arrogant young man say, "I opened a new church." I recall thinking to myself, I wonder if opening a new church necessarily equates to building the church. I think that some churches would be better left unopened. Have you ever considered that? We have too many churches that are filled with the wrong kind of people.

Jesus never said to go and make church members of all nations. Instead, He said to make disciples of all nations. (See Matthew 28:19.) A major problem in the church today is that our churches are filled with members who are not disciples.

Jesus said to go and make disciples—not church members—of all nations.

Jesus said to go into all the world, preaching the gospel to every creature, and that signs will follow those who believe. They will lay hands on the sick so that they recover, cast out demons, speak with new tongues, and so forth. (See Mark 16:17–18.) I have heard people say that the signs do not actually follow many believers, and this is why: the signs do not follow because the people do not go where God wants them to go. The signs follow those who go, and they have not been promised to any other group, especially a group of stationary people. As the saying goes, "It is hard to follow a parked car."

I once spent nine consecutive days in Pakistan, a country whose population is mostly Muslim. Christians were a tiny, oppressed, despised minority. However, God supernaturally enabled us to hold public meetings. During those nine days, the local Christians estimated that eighty-five hundred people prayed for salvation. At least one-third of these people were Muslims. We saw the most outstanding specific miracles I have ever witnessed in the course of my ministry. Very rarely have I seen the sense of hearing restored to a deaf person, or a crippled person healed, but in Pakistan, I witnessed both of these miracles.

The best place for a miracle is the worst of places.

The most incredible miracle of this experience was probably the healing of a Pakistani woman who was about sixty years old—she had been born blind, and she received perfect sight. We did not even lay hands on her; we merely prayed a collective prayer. It was impossible to lay hands on the throngs of people gathered there.

I tell you about this because I want to show, on the basis of personal experience, that signs do follow those who believe and go. You would be surprised what you could achieve with God if you would move out from where you are to a place where no one else goes. The best place for a miracle is the worst of places, for when there is no other way of obtaining results, God will provide a miracle.

While we were in Pakistan, I never felt the anointing of God in our meetings. Never was I "blessed." But God saw fit to honor our going with the miraculous.

My heart grieves over the multitudes of healthy, strong men and women who are merely eking out their lives in conventional Christianity when the world is crying out for what we have. In most places, you do not even need to persuade people to listen to you; they are eager and waiting to hear.

This is the harvest hour. Jesus said to pray that God would send forth laborers into the harvest. (See Matthew 9:38.) The word in Greek for *"send"* means *"thrust,"* and it is the same word in the New Testament used to talk about driving out demons. People must be "driven out" into the harvest by divine pressure. I pray that some of you will never be content until you are in the harvest. That is a challenge. People miss the call of God because they fail to listen.

Christians Must Serve the World

James 1:27 continues, *"Pure and undefiled religion before God and the Father is this: to visit orphans and widows in their trouble, and to keep oneself unspotted from the world."* This is God's view of religion.

How many "religious" people in the United States are practicing this form of *"pure and undefiled religion"*? Brothers and sisters, there is no shortage of orphans or widows. The Third World countries are filled with them. You can help them through one of many organizations that exist to reach out to them.

James 4:17 says, *"Therefore, to him who knows to do good and does not do it, to him it is sin."* I doubt whether God will charge us primarily with our sins of commission. Instead, it will be our sins of omission that He will admonish the most. We may have to sacrifice some personal convenience and give

204

up some of our time. Every now and then, we have to think of someone other than ourselves. What a revolution!

James 1:27 says, *"Visit orphans and widows in their trouble, and...keep oneself unspotted from the world."* The world is dirty. Every time we come in contact with it, we must cleanse ourselves. We must not let any of the dirty, greasy marks of the world soil our beautiful, white robe of righteousness in Christ. If we happen to get a greasy stain on our robes, there is only one detergent that cleans: the blood of Jesus.

The blood of Jesus is the only detergent that cleans the dirt of the world.

Have you ever tried to imagine what it would be like to be guilty and defiled without knowing where to go or what to do? To carry alone on your conscience the fact that you have done things of which you are ashamed, things you wished had never happened?

It is hard enough for a Christian to bear his conscience—and, after all, we can go straight to Jesus, confess, repent, and receive forgiveness, as if the sinful acts we committed never actually happened. Just imagine the agony of countless people burdened by their consciences but not knowing where to go! This is why we must *"preach the gospel to every creature"* (Mark 16:15).

Yet, again, we must interact with the world using discernment. In James 4:4, we read, *"Adulterers and adulteresses! Do you not know that friendship with the world is enmity with God? Whoever therefore wants to be a friend of the world makes himself an enemy of God."*

We cannot be on friendly terms with the system of this world. We can be friendly with our neighbors and show God's love to them, of course, but we must make sure not to fall in love with the system of the world, for it is wicked. The system of the world is controlled by the Prince of Darkness.

We Have Been Delivered

Philippians 3:17–21 reads,

Brethren, join in following my example, and note those who so walk, as you have us for a pattern. For many walk, of whom I have told you often, and now tell you even weeping, that they are the enemies of the cross of Christ: whose end is destruction, whose god is their belly, and whose glory is in their shame; who set their mind on earthly things. For our citizenship is in heaven, from which we also eagerly wait for the Savior, the Lord Jesus Christ, who will transform our lowly body that it may be conformed to His glorious body, according to the working by which He is able even to subdue all things to Himself.

We have been delivered from this present evil age because our citizenship is in heaven, the next age. Because we focus on the next age rather than the present one, we expect a Savior from heaven. Heaven, not earth, is where we have a home.

Where are we living, and in which age? What is our attitude toward the cross? Paul wrote, *"God forbid that I should boast except in the cross of our Lord Jesus Christ, by whom the world has been crucified to me, and I to the world"* (Galatians 6:14).

There is a dividing line between the church and the world. What stands between them? The cross of Christ. Again, we are on one side of the cross or the other. We can either say, like Paul, "I am crucified with Christ, who lives in me. The life that I live now in the flesh I live by the faith of the Son of God, who loved me and gave His life for me" (see Galatians 2:20), or we cannot.

If this nation contained forty million committed Christians, they would turn the nation upside down. But the few people who are earnestly trying to change things have one primary complaint: the church.

Brothers and sisters, I am supportive of pressuring the government to enact beneficial legislation, but I want to remind you that legislation does not change people's hearts. What this nation needs is a major change of heart—not only among the drug addicts and prostitutes, but also among the church-going believers. The Bible says the time has come for judgment, and judgment will begin at the house of God. (See 1 Peter 4:17.)

In the great move of the Holy Spirit known as the Welsh Revival, which transformed the nation of Wales in 1904, a primary instrument God used was a young man by the name of Evan Roberts. He used this slogan: "Bend the church and bow the world." If you can get the church to bend, you can cause the world to bow. But if the church will not bend, how can the world bow? There is one way to reach the world, and that is through the church. If the church resists the Holy Spirit, there is no way for the Holy Spirit to reach the world.

If the church will not bend, how can the world bow?

Where do we stand today? If you are willing, tell the Lord, "In the light of what Brother Prince has taught, I realize I have not been delivered from this present evil age, and I haven't had an inner transformation in my thinking, my values, or my motives God, I want You to change me. Whatever it takes, I want You to change me." God will take you at your word.

Despite Sufferings, We Have Overcome the World

As believers at odds with the world, we are guaranteed to meet with great difficulty. Jesus told His disciples, *"These things I have spoken to you, that in Me you may have peace. In the world you will have tribulation; but be of good cheer, I have over-come the world"* (John 16:33). Hallelujah

In the world, we will have tribulation. We may as well praise the Lord for it, because there will be no alleviation of tribulations if we do not praise Him. A dangerous kind of teaching is spreading that says if you encounter troubles and pressures, it means you are not living aligned with the will of God. This teaching is not necessarily true. When Paul and Barnabas spoke to a group of new converts in the cities they visited, they said, in effect, "Brethren, we must go through much tribulation to enter the kingdom of God. This is a hard fact of the Christian life." (See Acts 14:21–22.)

The guarantee of tribulation entails a piece of good news: through faith, believers have victory over the world.

For whatever is born of God overcomes the world. And this is the victory that has overcome the world; our faith. Who is he who overcomes the world, but he who believes that Jesus is the Son of God? (1 John 5:4–5)

The phrase *"overcome the world"* indicates a conflict with the world. We do not overcome something unless it stands in opposition to us. But we overcome the world by our faith when we exercise it.

Maintaining Focus

I have met many Christians who are easily distracted from focusing supremely on God. There are countless ways in which the devil can divert us from God's purpose for our lives. With whatever method works, Satan gets us out of line with God's purposes. Someone may not be a lost soul, but he or she may have a smaller reward in glory than he or she could have had.

Paul wrote to the church in Philippi about finishing his course, completing the objective to which God called him:

I press on, that I may lay hold of that for which Christ Jesus has also laid hold of me. Brethren, I do not count myself to have apprehended; but one thing I do, forgetting those things which are behind and reaching forward to those things which are ahead, I press toward the goal for the prize of the upward call of God in Christ Jesus. (Philippians 3:12–14)

I have done extensive biblical study concerning the requirements for fulfilling our calling in Christ, and I contend that they may be summed up in a single word: single-mindedness. If you become double-minded and allow your thinking to be diverted, you will not fulfill your calling.

The Cross: Our Means of Escape

I will close this chapter by relating a personal experience of particular relevance. In the mid-1950s I was serving as the pastor of a small Pentecostal congregation in the center of London. Three times weekly, we held street meetings in the middle of London, at a place called Speakers' Corner, Marble Arch. Preaching on the streets provides excellent training because you cannot rely on your notes or outlines. Extemporizing is essential, as is the ability to deal with hecklers and answer questions quickly.

During this period, I had a vivid dream in which I saw a typical street meeting—a circle of people stood and listened to a man in the center of the group. He was preaching with fervor. But as I looked at the man, I did not like what I saw. He was crooked, with a club foot and a hunched back. I said to myself, *What he is saying is good, but I do not like the way he looks.*

When I woke up, I thought nothing more of the dream until it recurred two weeks later. The repetition made me realize that God was trying to tell me something. I began to pray, describing the scene to the Lord and asking Him to identify the preacher. Who was the man? This question was answered in the same way the prophet Nathan answered David: *"Thou art the man"* (2 Samuel 12:7 KJV).

I realized that God was not criticizing my preaching, but He was looking at me, and He did not approve of what He saw. Meanwhile, I had been saved, baptized in the Holy Spirit, and could speak in tongues.

I was the criminal for whom the cross was made.

I began to think seriously about this dream. It was about Easter time, so the image of the three crosses on the hill of Golgotha was vivid in my mind. The middle cross was taller than the other two. As I turned this image over in my mind, the Holy Spirit seemed to talk to me, saying, "About that middle cross—for whom was it made?" And then He said, "Be careful before you answer."

I thought for a moment, then said, "It was made for Barabbas." He said, "That is right." I realized something that had never occurred to me before: the cross was there for Barabbas; it was waiting for him. But at the last moment, the Holy Spirit reminded me, Jesus took the place of Barabbas. "Yes," I affirmed.

I have been delivered from slavery to the world's opinions.

Then it hit me. I was the criminal for whom the cross was made. It was fashioned to my measure. It stood where I deserved to hang. My old man deserved nothing less than the cross, but Jesus took my place. My old man was crucified in Him.

I have not become perfect, but I am pressing upward toward the ultimate goal. I am not static or stuck in a rut. I am not a slave to traditions; I do not care what the world says or thinks. What matters to me is what God thinks. I have been delivered from slavery to the opinions of this world.

Paul said, in effect, "Through the cross, the world is crucified to me, and I am crucified to the world." (See Galatians 6:14.) In other words, Paul said that when the world looked at him, all they saw was a corpse hanging on a cross.

When Paul looked at the world, he saw the same thing—a corpse hanging on a cross. That was the value of the world to him; it held no valuable charms. It did not impress him with its wealth, knowledge, or power, all of which are passing away. A new kingdom is coming—a kingdom that is not of this world. This kingdom is where I belong. It is the kingdom of my true, eternal citizenship.

Do we desire release from the slavery of the flesh and the world? There is one way out: the cross. Those who belong to Christ have crucified the flesh, along with its passions and desires. The world is crucified to me, and I to the world.

Thank God for the cross! If it were not for the cross, we would be slaves forever. The cross is our way to freedom. It is not a pain-free way, but *"he who has suffered in the flesh has ceased from sin"* (1 Peter 4:1). We can reach the point where we are so sick of our flesh that it can no longer tempt us to sin.

DELIVERED FROM
THIS PRESENT EVIL AGE

The word *"age"* is the translation given in the *King James Bible* of two distinct words appearing frequently in the New Testament. In newer versions, one of these words is translated as *"age,"* the other as *"world."*

I will not delve too deeply into a Greek lesson, but the word translated *"age"* is *aion* in Greek, from which we derive the English word *eon*. The meaning is nearly identical.

For now, we will focus on the word translated as *"age"*— *aion* (or *eon*). We will begin this study of the age, or ages, in the first chapter of Galatians.

> *Grace to you and peace from God the Father and our Lord Jesus Christ, who gave Himself for our sins, that He might deliver us from this present evil age, according to the will of our God and Father.* (verses 3–4)

We see in this passage that one primary purpose for which Jesus died was to deliver us from this *"present evil age."* Have you ever evaluated the authenticity of your deliverance from this age? I doubt that many Christians think in such terms. We live in this age, after all—how could we be delivered from it? But the purpose of the death of Jesus was indeed to deliver us—to rescue us—from this present evil age.

The New Testament abounds with references to ages. In Hebrews 1:1–2, we read, *"God, who at various times and in different ways spoke in time past to the fathers by the prophets, has in these last days spoken to us by His Son."* This Son, *"whom He has appointed heir of all things,"* (verse 2) is the conclusion of everything.

It is typical of the book of Hebrews to put the end before the beginning, because the theme of the entire book is the process of perfection. This book was written for Jewish believers who, though they had a thorough knowledge of the Scriptures, were not moving forward in God to become more like Him. I think Gentile believers today require the same message. Again, the thrust of Hebrews is the call to go on to perfection—to move into our inheritance and our ultimate rest. These three key words encapsulate the theme of Hebrews: perfection, rest, and inheritance.

Jesus died to rescue us from this present evil age.

Verse 2 establishes Jesus' role as the heir of all things. It goes on to describe the creative nature of Jesus, *"through whom also He* [God] *made the world* [Greek, aion]...." Some translations say *"worlds,"* but the Greek word means *ages*.

We learn next that He was *"the brightness of His* [the Father's] *glory and the express image of His person* [substance]," who upholds *"all things by the word of His power"* (verse 3). These are five eternal facts regarding the divine nature of

Jesus. The last two facts pertain to His redemptive work: *"He had by Himself purged our sins..."* and He *"sat down at the right hand of the Majesty on high"* (verse 3).

Each of these statements invites an in-depth examination, but I would like to focus on the second statement: that God made the ages through Jesus. The King James Version translates the word for *"ages"* as *world*, which seems to make better sense because, to us, the word *"ages"* implies the concept of time, while the word *worlds* implies the concepts of matter and space.

Visible Temporality, Invisible Eternity

God created the ages, setting all time in motion in relation to space. Note that the word is plural, *"ages,"* not singular or referring to one single age.

A similar statement worth noting comes in Hebrews 11:3: *"By faith we understand that the worlds were framed by the word of God, so that the things which are seen were not made of things which are visible."* Once again, we find that the biblical text aligns with modern physics. Ask a physicist what a desk consists of, and he or she will answer in terms of protons, neutrons, electrons, and other fundamental components—none of which has ever been seen by the human eye. Is it not remarkable that the writer of Hebrews—someone lacking modern scientific knowledge—was still in complete harmony with contemporary scientific conclusions?

God brought the ages into being by His Word—something that is not visible—so that everything visible, everything material, everything we consider "real" or tangible was made out of something that we cannot see. What cannot be seen is the ultimate, eternal reality, while everything that can be seen is only a temporary reality.

The apostle Paul affirmed this truth in his second epistle to the church at Corinth: *"We do not look at the things which are seen, but at the things which are not seen. For the things which are seen are temporary, but the things which are not seen are eternal"* (2 Corinthians 4:18). This counterintuitive concept demands a mental revolution. Again, the Bible says that what we perceive or observe with our five senses is only temporary; the realities that endure, such as faith, hope, and love, are invisible.

> *What we perceive with our senses is temporary.*

The book of Revelation includes several somber passages that deal with this temporary age as well. We read of God's coming judgment of Babylon, representative of the false church, in Revelation 19:3: *"Again they said, 'Alleluia! Her smoke rises up forever and ever!'"* For generations, the universe will never lack a reminder of the consequences of rebelling against God. The smoke will serve as a continual reminder.

Revelation 20:10 speaks of the devil and the Antichrist: *"The devil, who deceived them, was cast into the lake of fire and brimstone where the beast and the false prophet are. And they will be tormented day and night forever and ever."* Their torment will endure forever.

These issues are rather solemn, are they not? No one would wish to suffer torment for the duration of the ages, but if we cast our lot with Satan and join his camp, we will end in the same place he will.

Revelation 22:5 says, *"There shall be no night there: They need no lamp nor light of the sun, for the Lord God gives them light. And they shall reign forever and ever."* Who are the *"they"* this passage mentions? They are God's servants. (See verse 3.) If we receive Christ as Lord and Savior and are serving God, we shall reign with Him forever.

God's servants shall reign with Him forever.

When Jesus came to earth as the Savior two millennia ago, He came at the consummation of the ages. Hebrews 9:26 points out that Jesus did not have to offer Himself as a sacrifice more than one time, because *"He then would have had to suffer often since the foundation of the world; but now, once at the end of the ages, He has appeared to put away sin by the sacrifice of Himself."*

The phrase *"the end of the ages"* is translated in the *New American Standard Bible* as *"the consummation of the ages."* This means the weaving together of everything, the convergence of everything to its close. When Jesus came, it was to bring all the ages of God's purposes to their consummation for the final, complete resolution of all the purposes of God.

217

The Implications of Jesus' Coming

In the last chapter, we discussed what the New Testament says about the eternal implications of Jesus' coming. The New Testament also speaks about the implications of the end of the ages for us.

Paul wrote about the experiences of the Israelites as they traveled from Egypt into the land of Canaan, encountering troubles and committing sins along the way: *"Now all these things happened to them as examples, and they were written for our admonition, upon whom the ends of the ages have come"* (1 Corinthians 10:11).

This passage attributes great significance to us, does it not? The ends of the ages have come upon us; the unfolding of all of God's eternal purposes rests, in some sense, on us. As Christians who believe in God, we must never underestimate our importance, because all of God's eternal purposes focus on us and the times in which we live.

Underestimating ourselves is among the worst things we can do. First of all, we are God's handiwork. He designed and created us, and any time we criticize ourselves, we criticize by extension Him who made us. We have no right to do so.

Focus

Second, by God's grace, we are the most significant factor in the universe. His purposes center on us, and if we truly grasp this truth, we will find it impossible to lead a life of idle triviality. One day, we will answer to God for what became of His purposes. We will all answer to God, and this reality attests to our importance.

This Age Is Ending

An important fact we must grasp is that the present age is approaching its end. Do you live with this belief, or do you live as if the end is not near? Countless Scripture passages in the New Testament tell us that the present age is passing away, reaching its end; it will not continue indefinitely. This is reason to be thankful, because this world is a mess, quite frankly. Moreover, the mess is getting worse.

> *God's purposes center on us; we cannot lead lives of idle triviality.*

In the book of Matthew, Jesus spoke metaphorically about the end of this age with an analogy about the harvest of wheat and tares. *"The enemy who sowed them* [the tares] *is the devil, the harvest is the end of the age, and the reapers are the angels. Therefore as the tares are gathered and burned in the fire, so it will be at the end of this age"* (Matthew 13:39–40). Verse 49 continues, *"So it will be at the end of the age. The angels will come forth,* [and] *separate the wicked from among the just."*

The disciples asked Jesus, *"Tell us,…what will be the sign of Your coming, and of the end of the age?"* (Matthew 24:3). Jesus did not correct them and say, "This age is not going to end." Rather, He answered them specifically (see verses 4–31) and exhorted them, saying, *"He who endures to the end shall be saved"* (verse 13). The end will come, but not before specific things come to pass. Jesus instructed His followers about how they should live until then, recorded in Matthew 28:19–20:

> *Go therefore and make disciples of all the nations, baptiz-*
> *ing them in the name of the Father and of the Son and of*
> *the Holy Spirit, teaching them to observe all things that I*
> *have commanded you; and lo, I am with you always, even*
> *to the end of the age.* This WAS A command

If you are living as though this age will never end, you must adjust your lifestyle. You are living in a false system of improper values and misplaced priorities.

Jesus' Name Is Eternally Supreme

The next fact is exciting: the name of Jesus is supreme in this age and in the next; that will never change:

> *He [God] raised Him [Jesus] from the dead and seated*
> *Him at His right hand in the heavenly places, far above*
> *all principality and power and might and dominion, and*
> *every name that is named, not only in this age but also in*
> *that which is to come.* (Ephesians 1:20–21)

My Jesus is sitting along side of God

Again, Paul looked past the present age to the next, saying that although this age will end, nothing will change the position or the significance of Jesus. He has been, is, and will be there for the ages of the ages.

Too often the church of today forgets that in the present age, Satan is the ruler. Paul spoke about this in his second epistle to the church at Corinth:

But even if our gospel is veiled, it is veiled to those who are perishing, whose minds the god of this age has blinded, who do not believe, lest the light of the gospel of the glory of Christ, who is the image of God, should shine on them.

(2 Corinthians 4:3–4)

Satan is *"the god of this age,"* which is one reason that he does not want this age to end. He is doing everything he can to prolong this present age, for when it ends, he will cease to be a god; his status will be demoted.

While Satan is not equal to God, humanity has made him a god by agreeing with him, rebelling against the true God, and replacing Him with false gods. This age is evil because it has Satan as its ruler.

God's ultimate plan is not to change this age but to bring it to an end. Christians who direct all of their efforts toward changing this age are misguided. There are many things that we are able and ought to change, but we must bear in mind that every change we effect in this age will not be permanent, for the age is reaching its end.

The Current World Order Is Temporary

The New Testament talks about not loving the world. (See 1 John 2:15.) This does not mean that we are not to love God's creation or that we are not to love people; rather, it means that there is a certain world system that we are not to love because it is the total enemy of God. If we love God's enemies, we are traitors to God.

For example, 2 Peter 2:5 says, "[God] *did not spare the ancient world, but saved Noah, one of eight people, a preacher of righteousness, bringing in the flood on the world of the ungodly."*

222

Speaking still of the flood, 2 Peter 3:6 says, *"The world that then existed perished, being flooded with water."*

What perished in the flood was the world order of Noah's day. It was not the earth that perished; rather, it was a certain social system that was called *"the world."* You must understand that this is what the Bible is generally referring to when it talks about *"the world."*

Satan Rules the World System

Man's fall made Satan *"the ruler of this world."* He does not rule the universe, but he does rule the present world system. Jesus gave this title to Satan three times in the book of John. In John 12:31, Jesus said, *"Now is the judgment of this world; now the ruler of this world will be cast out."* The title *"ruler of this world"* recurs in John 16:11, where Jesus said, *"The ruler of this world is cast out."* Again speaking of judgment, Jesus said in John 14:30, *"The ruler of this world is coming, and he has nothing in Me."* Therein lies the secret of Jesus' victory, and our victory, too, when we have been born again and Jesus Christ lives in us.

Satan could not defeat Jesus because Jesus said, *"He has nothing in Me."* If you and I can say, *"He has nothing in me,"* we are unconquerable.　he has nothing in me.

Enemy within the Gates

Have you heard the phrase "the fifth column"? It was used frequently before and during World War II, and its origins are particularly interesting. In 1936, during the civil war in Spain, a Spanish general was leading an attack on a city occupied by his opponents.

Another general came to him and asked, "General, what is your plan to take the city?"

The first general answered, "I have four columns advancing on the city—one from the north, one from the east, one from the south, and one from the west." He paused, then added, "But it is my fifth column that I expect to take the city for me."

The second general said, "Where is your fifth column?"

The response: "Inside the city."

The fifth column comprised traitors who would ultimately undermine the city's defenses. This is exactly how Satan defeats individuals and the church: never from without, but from within. Unless we can say, "He has nothing in me," we are in danger.

Dominion by Deception

The next point we must understand about Satan's tactics is that he does control the world system via deception, as I have elaborated in earlier chapters. Without successfully deceiving people, Satan could not control them.

A vote against God elects Satan as your ruler.

We find a most remarkable statement in 1 John 5:19: *"We know that we are of God, and the whole world lies under the sway of the wicked one."* While the *New King James Version* says *"under the sway,"* the literal Greek meaning of this statement is, "The whole world lies in the wicked one." Satan, *"the wicked one,"* has the whole world in his grasp.

We all know the children's song whose lyrics say that the Lord has the "whole world in His hands," but I do not think this song is scripturally sound. It is not the Lord, but Satan, who has the world in his grasp. While the Lord is supreme over everything, including Satan, Satan still controls the world, however temporarily.

Revelation 12:9 speaks of what the church must eventually do to the devil. It reads, *"So the great dragon was cast out, that serpent of old, called the Devil and Satan, who deceives the whole world."* It speaks of the inhabited globe, the residents of which are deceived by Satan.

Ruler of the Rebels

Satan rules over all rebels; thus, those who rebel against God are under the dominion of Satan. You do not have to vote for Satan. All that is required is a vote against God; the moment you do that, even if only in your heart, you elect Satan by default as your ruler.

Ephesians 2:1–3 says,

You [believers in Christ] *He made alive, who were dead in trespasses and sins, in which you once walked according to the course of this world, according to the prince of the power of the air, the spirit who now works in the sons of disobedience, among whom also we all once conducted ourselves in the lusts of our flesh, fulfilling the desires of the flesh and of the mind, and were by nature children of wrath, just as the others.*

This passage begins by talking about when we were dead—not physically, but spiritually. It mentions a time when we all *"conducted ourselves in the lusts of our flesh."* The word translated *"flesh"* is what we call the "natural man," or "unregenerate man"—someone who has not been born again and therefore is not yet transformed by the grace of God, but who is instead subject to the dominion of Satan. This dominion is a spiritual force that works in him because of his rebellious nature.

It works through the lusts and uncontrollable desires of his fleshly nature and mind. The enmity, or hostility, of the unregenerate man is just as strong in his mind as in his body. As Paul wrote in Romans 8:7, *"The carnal mind is enmity against God."*

The passage concludes by saying that we *"were by nature children of wrath"* (Ephesians 2:3). But we are all by nature children of God's wrath because we are children of disobedience. We share one ancestor who was disobedient, and that was Adam. Because we inherited Adam's sinful nature, we fall under Satan's dominion, and we depend on God to deliver us from it.

Not Siding with Satan

The forty-first chapter of Job speaks of a creature known as Leviathan. This monstrous creature is actually a picture of Satan. We learn, *"He [Leviathan] beholds every high thing; he is king over all the children of pride"* (Job 41:34).

All proud people have a king whose name is Satan.

All proud people have a king, though they may not know it. His name is Satan. The moment you say, "I know best; I can make my own way through life; I can handle this situation; I do not want to depend on God," you elect Leviathan as your king. That is the condition of the world, the kingdom of Satan.

226

Satan claims to control the kingdoms and governments of this world. We read this in Luke about the devil's temptation of Jesus:

Then the devil, taking Him [Jesus] up on a high mountain, showed Him all the kingdoms of the world in a moment of time. And the devil said to Him, "All this authority I will give You, and their glory; for this has been delivered to me, and I give it to whomever I wish." (Luke 4:5–6)

Satan says that all the world has been delivered to him. The word used here for *"delivered"* is the same word that was used to describe Judas's betrayal of Jesus to the rulers of the Jews. Satan essentially said to Jesus, "All of this has been betrayed to me." Who was responsible for this betrayal? Who was responsible for handing over the rule of the earth to the devil? Adam was. He defied God and sided with Satan, handing over to him the authority God originally gave to Adam. Satan thus claims to control all kingdoms and governments. And he certainly does control most of them.

The Good News Is...

If we focus only on the evil in the world and on the activity of Satan, our view will be quite unchristian. In spite of widespread evil in the world, and in spite of the world's rebellion, pride, and arrogance, God loves the world. He loves the world so much, in fact, that He gave His Son, Jesus Christ, to die for it. *"For God so loved the world that He gave His only begotten Son, that whoever believes in Him should not perish but have everlasting life"* (John 3:16).

We are all so very arrogant, and I marvel that God could ever love me. I truly do. I have never been able to understand it, but I have had to believe it. If we do not grasp this truth, we will be out of line with all of God's purposes.

Although God had every right and reason to condemn the world to destruction in an instant, He does not have the attitude we likely would, were we to have His power. Despite its rebellion, God loves the world and gave His Son, Jesus Christ, to die for it. The ultimate result of the cross was Satan's defeat.

Accomplishments of the Cross

The cross was God's judgment on Satan and on the world. Jesus said, *"Now is the judgment of this world; now the ruler of this world will be cast out"* (John 12:31). Satan rules the world, but the cross set limits on the bounds of his dominion.

Jesus went on to say, *"And I, if I am lifted up from the earth, will draw all peoples to Myself"* (verse 32). It is clear that Jesus was speaking about the cross.

The cross set limits on Satan's dominion.

You see, Satan believed that he was getting Jesus crucified and thereby securing victory. That was the biggest mistake he ever made. Satan's perceived victory—Jesus' suffering on the cross— proved to be Satan's ultimate defeat, for Jesus' death on the cross judged Satan and the social world order he rules over. Jesus suffered in the place of guilty humanity, enduring the punishment due to the world and saving those who are born again.

Romans 6:6 informs us, *"Our old man was crucified with Him."* When we look at the cross, we are looking at God's

228

estimate of our unregenerate nature. It contains not even one ounce of goodness. As Paul wrote in Romans 7:18, *"For I know that in me (that is, in my flesh) nothing good dwells."* The difference between Paul and some of us is that Paul knew that apart from Christ, no goodness is within us.

We dwell in safety on the correct side of the cross.

The mercy of God is that the judgment of the cross was enacted in Jesus. His crucifixion enacted God's judgment and set boundaries on Satan's territory, giving Christians the power to stay out of it. I like to think of the cross as God's red light or stop sign. When Satan is driving up against us, he sees that stop sign, slams on his brakes, and squeals to a stop, because he cannot get beyond our belief in the cross and the redemptive work of the blood of Jesus.

We dwell in safety when we dwell on the correct side of the cross. In John 16:8–11, Jesus said,

> *When He* [the Holy Spirit] *has come, He will convict the world of sin, and of righteousness, and of judgment: of sin, because they do not believe in Me; of righteousness, because I go to My Father and you see Me no more; of judgment, because the ruler of this world is judged.*

Open Defeat for Satan

Satan, the ruler of this world, *"is judged."* Through the cross, God administered to Satan a total, irreversible, eternal defeat that Satan can never change.

> *You, being dead in your trespasses and the uncircumcision of your flesh, He has made alive together with Him, having forgiven you all trespasses, having wiped out the*

handwriting of requirements that was against us, which was contrary to us. And He has taken it out of the way, having nailed it to the cross. Having disarmed principalities and powers, He made a public spectacle of them, triumphing over them in it. (Colossians 2:13–15)

Note this!

The cross stripped Satan of his weapons, put him to an open defeat, and made a public display of him. We need to know this vital truth, but Satan will do all that he can to keep the church ignorant of what the cross actually accomplished.

In Galatians 3:1, Paul wrote, *"O foolish Galatians! Who has bewitched you that you should not obey the truth, before whose eyes Jesus Christ was clearly portrayed among you as crucified?"* He was addressing Spirit-filled Christians who had experienced miracles but were now *"bewitched."* They were blinded to the truth of the cross.

Blinding us is among Satan's primary objectives, because once we lose sight of the cross, we become Satan's pawns or playthings. The only way to victory is through the knowledge and affirmation of what the cross accomplished.

God's Answer: The Cross

In this wicked world, God's answer is the cross. The only response to the evils and pressures and claims of this world is to apply the blood of Jesus shed on the cross in your life. Galatians 5:24 says, *"Those who are Christ's have crucified the flesh with its passions and desires."* Christians—we who belong to Christ, regardless of our denominations—have crucified the flesh with its passions and desires.

God's provision is always two-sided, comprising what God has done and also what we must do.

Romans 6:6 says, *"Our old man was crucified with Him [Jesus]."* When Jesus died on the cross, our unregenerate man was judged. Jesus incurred the judgment deserved by the criminal within you and me. When you look at the cross, you see where you should have been. Our old nature was crucified along with Christ, yet God's provision in Jesus must be applied to each individual life. Those who belong to Christ have crucified the flesh, having taken their position with Him on the cross. They echo Paul's words in Galatians 2:20:

> *I have been crucified with Christ; it is no longer I who live, but Christ lives in me; and the life which I now live in the flesh I live by faith in the Son of God, who loved me and gave Himself for me.*

This confession personalizes the accomplishment of the cross. The cross works in our lives and wipes out our sin when we make the right confession and believe it in our hearts. (See Psalm 103:11–12; Micah 7:19; Hebrews 8:12.)

The Rest of the Story

The work of the cross is multifaceted. First, it involves what God has done for us through Jesus' death on the cross. We rejoice in that truth, but it is not the end of the story.

Second, the cross involves what it must do within us. Our old nature must die. God has provided the means of this death, but Jesus said that any man who will follow Him must do two things: deny himself and take up his cross. (See Matthew 16:24; Mark 8:34; Luke 9:23.)

What does our cross consist of? I will provide two definitions. First, our cross is the place where our will and God's

231

will intersect. If we follow Jesus, we will come to this place. Second, our cross is the place where we "die." God does not impose this death on us; rather, we accept this death if we want to. We can choose not to die, but we cannot follow Jesus unless we do.

Our cross is the place where our will and God's will intersect.

If you are having trouble following Jesus, perhaps you have not taken up your cross. We can consider the cross an instrument of torture and execution, or we can consider the cross a way of release from our old nature. Thank God that He provides a way out!

In Romans 7:24, Paul lamented, *"O wretched man that I am! Who will deliver me from this body of death?"* His answer is immediate and filled with gratitude: *"I thank God; through Jesus Christ our Lord!"* (verse 25). God gives us a way out through Jesus Christ, but we will not take that way out until we perceive our need for it.

Much of the struggle we endure in our Christian life comes as God tries to convince us that we need the cross. The earlier we are convicted of this necessity, the more successful we will be as Christians.

Even More

The cross achieved even more. Galatians 6:14 says, *"God forbid that I should boast except in the cross of our Lord Jesus Christ, by whom the world has been crucified to me, and I to the world."* Paul denied having anything to boast about—not even about being a descendant of Abraham, being a Pharisee, keeping the law, or establishing churches. He had nothing to boast about, except for one thing: the cross of our Lord Jesus Christ.

This statement is incredible, especially because in Roman culture, the cross was a despicable object. Yet it was what Paul chose to boast about for all of eternity! Through the cross, the world had been crucified to Paul, and Paul to the world.

The world has no claim on the other side of the cross. Its territory ends at the cross, as do its pressures and temptations. On the other side of the cross is peace—peace at a price, however. The price is our own death. Yet as we die to ourselves, we go on living. How? It is not we who are living, but Christ who lives in us. (See Galatians 2:20.)

Birth of a New Kingdom

This process of the advent of the new kingdom that God enacts within us will also happen to the world order. God is not going to change the world; He is going to replace it. In Matthew 19:28, Jesus said, *"Assuredly I say to you, that in the regeneration, when the Son of Man sits on the throne of His glory, you who have followed Me will also sit on twelve thrones, judging the twelve tribes of Israel."*

God will not change the world; He will replace it.

The word for *"regeneration"* is the same word used to refer to the process of being born again. A new world order will be born, for how else can we enter the kingdom of God but through a birth? Individuals and the human race alike must experience a birth to bring the kingdom.

This birth will bring about a new age. The present age is passing away, and God will not patch it up. No, He is going to replace it with a new order that will be born on earth. I believe we are living through the labor pains of this birthing process.

When a young wife becomes pregnant and nine months have elapsed, she begins to have cramps and labor pains. Does her husband say, "I wish we could get rid of these pains"? No! He realizes that the labor pains must run their course for the baby to be born, so he takes his wife to the hospital.

Similarly, you are not going to stop the labor pains of this earth by trying to stitch the broken world together again. It is foolish to try to stop the pains. All we can do is seek the birth.

God is establishing a kingdom that is not of this world. In John 18:36, Jesus told Pilate, *"My kingdom is not of this world. If My kingdom were of this world, My servants would fight, so that I should not be delivered to the Jews; but now My kingdom is not from here."*

I do not believe Christians should fight to establish the kingdom of God. A Christian may be obligated to give military service to his country, but he does not fight to establish the kingdom of God.

The kingdom comes not through a battle, but through a birth—a birth that will bring about judgment on the world, cutting through the veil of deception to expose and separate true from false believers, the true Christ from the Antichrist, the true church from the false church, and securing Christ's final, eternal victory.

CONCLUSION

In 2 Thessalonians 2, Paul wrote about the return of Jesus in power and glory to establish His kingdom on earth in place of the world's system:

Now, brethren, concerning the coming of our Lord Jesus Christ and our gathering together to Him, we ask you, not to be soon shaken in mind or troubled, either by spirit or by word or by letter, as if from us, as though the day of Christ had come. (verses 1–2)

In other words, do not believe it when people tell you that the day of the Lord has come. People were already making this claim in Paul's day; some even circulated forged letters to this effect, pretending they were penned by Paul.

Paul continued his warning, "*Let no one deceive you by any means; for that Day will not come unless the falling away comes first, and the man of sin is revealed, the son of perdition*" (verse 3). The coming of the Lord will not happen until an apostasy; some to whom the truth has been revealed will reject it. Rejection necessitates initial reception, and where else can this occur but in the church, where the truth has been taught and received? In addition, the identity of the Antichrist will be known before the coming of the Lord. Keep this in mind.

The True Church

The true church is the great bulwark that protects the world from the Antichrist. But when the false church falls away from the true—when it succumbs to Satan's deception and breaks faithfulness to God—the bulwark will crumble, opening the way for the Antichrist to be revealed.

The false church's falling away factors into Satan's strategy to unveil the Antichrist. This is why we must learn to keep the two churches distinct and remain personally faithful to Christ.

Opposition will increase, but those who endure to the end will be saved. God will use the Antichrist's evil activities to refine the true church and bring forth a pure bride for the Lord Jesus Christ. Scripture declares that Christ's bride, the true church, will be glorious, holy, spotless, and without blemish. (See Ephesians 5:27.)

Those who endure to the end will be saved.

The Lord will lavish His love and blessing on His bride, the true church. Those who belong to the true church will share His throne throughout eternity. The false church, on the other hand, will be cast aside and rejected, a forgotten relic of history.

Our Relationship with Jesus

Belonging to the true church is not a question of whether we prophesy or speak in tongues; it does not matter what particular mode of baptism we received or how many Scripture passages we have memorized. Rather, what matters is our personal relationship with Jesus Christ. Is He the Lord of our lives? Are we completely committed to Him? We prove our membership in the true church when we honor and serve the Lord, taking a stand for Him even in the face of opposition and persecution. We must put aside denominational labels

Love the truth; God will protect you from delusion.

and instead ask ourselves if we will we be faithful to Jesus.

We must resist the devil, repent of our sins, and submit to God, thereby thwarting Satan's dominion. If we love the truth, God will protect us from delusion.

A Closing Prayer

Pray this prayer with me:

Heavenly Father, we come to You in the name of the Lord Jesus Christ, our wonderful Savior and our Lord. We thank You for the great salvation that You have purchased for us through the blood of Your Son. We do not take our salvation lightly. We thank You for the guidance You provide in the Scriptures, and we desire to live our lives according to what they teach us. We humble ourselves before You and acknowledge our total dependence upon You; it is only by Your faithfulness and mercy that we will be preserved.

Lord, we commit ourselves to You. We renounce any area in which deception may have gained some ground in our lives. We turn against it and drive it from us, loosening ourselves from its grasp in the name of Jesus.

We embrace the truth that is Jesus, the truth that is the Scriptures, and the truth that is the Holy Spirit. We open our hearts and minds to You, asking You to fill us with Your truth.

In Jesus' name, amen.

Derek Prince (1915–2003) was born in Bangalore, India, into a British military family. He was educated as a scholar of classical languages (Greek, Latin, Hebrew, and Aramaic) at Eton College and Cambridge University in England and later at Hebrew University, Israel. As a student, he was a philosopher and self-proclaimed atheist. He held a fellowship in ancient and modern philosophy at King's College, Cambridge.

While in the British Medical Corps during World War II, Prince began to study the Bible as a philosophical work. Converted through a powerful encounter with Jesus Christ, he was baptized in the Holy Spirit a few days later. This life-changing experience altered the whole course of his life, which he thereafter devoted to studying and teaching the Bible as the Word of God.

Discharged from the army in Jerusalem in 1945, he married Lydia Christensen, founder of a children's home there. Upon their marriage, he immediately became father to Lydia's eight adopted daughters—six Jewish, one Palestinian Arab, and one English. Together, the family saw the rebirth of the state of Israel in 1948. In the late 1950s, the Princes adopted another daughter while Derek was serving as principal of a college in Kenya.

In 1963, the Princes immigrated to the United States and pastored a church in Seattle. Stirred by the tragedy of John F. Kennedy's assassination, Prince began to teach Americans how to intercede for their nation. In 1973, he became one of the founders of Intercessors for America. His book *Shaping History through Prayer and Fasting* has awakened Christians around the world to their responsibility to pray for their governments. Many consider underground translations of the book as instrumental in the fall of communist regimes in the USSR, East Germany, and Czechoslovakia.

Lydia Prince died in 1975, and Derek married Ruth Baker (a single mother to three adopted children) in 1978. He met his second wife, like the first, while he was serving the Lord in Jerusalem. Ruth died in December 1998 in Jerusalem, where they had lived since 1981.

Until a few years before his own death in 2003 at the age of eighty-eight, Prince persisted in the ministry God had called him to as he traveled the world, imparting God's revealed truth, praying for the sick and afflicted, and sharing his prophetic insights into world events in the light of Scripture. He wrote more than fifty books, which have been translated into more than sixty languages and distributed worldwide. He pioneered teaching on such groundbreaking themes as generational curses, the biblical significance of Israel, and demonology.

Derek Prince Ministries, with its international headquarters in Charlotte, North Carolina, continues to distribute his teachings and to train missionaries, church leaders, and congregations through its worldwide branch offices. Prince's radio program, *Keys to Successful Living* (now known as *Derek Prince Legacy Radio*), began in 1979 and has been translated into more than a dozen languages. Estimates are that Derek Prince's clear, nondenominational, nonsectarian teaching of the Bible has reached more than half the globe.

Internationally recognized as a Bible scholar and spiritual patriarch, Derek Prince established a teaching ministry that spanned six continents and more than sixty years. In 2002, he said, "It is my desire—and I believe the Lord's desire—that this ministry continue the work, which God began through me over sixty years ago, until Jesus returns."